THE ESSENCE OF BRUCKNER

Anton Bruckner in 1896

THE ESSENCE OF BRUCKNER

An essay towards the understanding of
his music

by

ROBERT SIMPSON

CHILTON BOOK COMPANY
Philadelphia New York London

Published in Philadelphia, 1968,
by Chilton Book Company
Copyright © 1967 by Robert Simpson
First American Edition   All Rights Reserved
Library of Congress Catalog Card Number 68–28040
Printed in Great Britain by
The Camelot Press Ltd., London and Southampton

To
JASCHA HORENSTEIN
who interprets Bruckner with love and authority

CONTENTS

CONTENTS

PREFACE

This book attempts to consider Bruckner through the ears of a composer; I am no musicologist, nor biographer, nor (in the common meaning of the term) critic. It is my belief that the inner processes of music reveal themselves most readily to another sympathetic composer, and since Bruckner's music has moved and fascinated me for some twenty-five years, I feel at last able to try to describe some of the things I have found in it. It has been a great pleasure to see the progress that Bruckner has made in the English-speaking countries since the war, for I have only too vivid memories of the bad old days when it was nearly impossible to find anyone who would look seriously at his scores. Naturally welcoming the change, I am still at a loss to explain it, for the music is the same; though I am now more critical of it than I was in the days of rash youth, it is the same innocent grandeur that still excites my admiration, and I have never been able to fathom why just as many people should not have appreciated it then as do now. Such qualities do not alter with time or fashion; we hear airy theories about climates of opinion, but where do such climates originate? Not, I think, in the mass of music lovers, who tend to react to what they are given and who learn to accept most of what is offered frequently and regularly enough, provided it is not too unkind. I suspect (to use no stronger a word) that it is the purveyors of opinion in the press who are mainly responsible. Concert promoters were unwilling to risk Bruckner while most of the critics were hostile to him, while the public were continually being told that it was a waste of time to go and hear him. Now that the "climate" has changed (in other words, now that all the old journalists are dead or retired, and new ones have taken over with different views), the risk is no longer serious and the number of Bruckner performances is rapidly increasing. We can only hope that the present incumbents will have long and preferably silent lives.

In the chapters that follow I have not hesitated to use previously published material of my own wherever I have been unable to find better words; all such matter is here revised, and elaborated or clarified. The largest such portions are the chapters on the Seventh and

Eighth symphonies, the former originally written for *Music Review* and the latter for *Chord and Discord*, the magazine of the Bruckner Society of America; both have been somewhat expanded. Other passages and expressions will also be found in a booklet I wrote for the B.B.C. in 1963, again sometimes changed, I hope for the better, and I have occasionally drawn on various programme notes. But most of the book, by far the greater part, is entirely new.

Chearsley, October 1966   R. S.

CHAPTER I

EMERGENCE

THE STRANGE CASE of Anton Bruckner almost defeats the imagin-ation. If we consider the stories of his legendary personal naïvety, his primitive provincial background, his total lack of general culture, his constant failure to grasp even moderately intelligent ideas about life, either in writing or in conversation, his absurd gullibility, his helpless shyness, sometimes resulting in quite appalling obsequiousness, his curious mania for counting objects, and many other evidences of his inadequacy in the eyes of the brilliant and often derisive intellectual circles of Vienna, we may well wonder how such a creature could have become an artist of any kind. But that he should have been a composer of works so immense, so original, and so controversial as to have aroused the highest devotion and hostility in opposite musical camps, may seem incredible. In this study I do not propose either to recount stale anecdotes or to attempt an explanation of the extraordinary phenomenon; Bruckner's music has suffered too much because his critics have known more about his pathetic life than was good for their artistic judgment, and my chief purpose is to examine the musical mind that gave rise to the only thing left to us—the music itself.

During the course of this book we shall have to scotch some old wives' tales, and will do well to start with the one that tells how Bruckner suddenly became a composer of genius at the age of forty, or thereabouts. Now it is true that his first masterpieces, the D minor and E minor masses and the First Symphony, were all written at that time, in the 1860s, but it is too often asserted that everything he wrote earlier showed no more than average ability, and sometimes less than that. He was in fact twelve when he began to compose, in 1836; this was a year after he had been sent to Hörsching (near Linz) by his schoolmaster father to study organ and composition under his cousin J. B. Weiss, and even then he was considered to show more than usual promise. I am not going to embark on biographical detail that is available in other books, but we should take note that by the time he was twenty he had written two and a half masses and a number of smaller choral works, and had already proved himself a brilliant organist with striking powers of improvisation. At twenty-five, in

1849, he wrote the Requiem in D minor, a work that could well bear revival, showing an artistic restraint blended with a quiet boldness that would do credit to any promising composer of that age. Most of his early works are church music, resulting from his education at the monastery of St. Florian; this superb Baroque building, one of the largest and finest in Europe, dominates the country near Linz. Ansfelden, the village where Bruckner was born in 1824, lies almost under its shadow and Windhaag and Kronstorf, the small places where he taught in local schools, are not very far away; even in Vienna, where he spent the last twenty-eight years of his life, Bruckner was never mentally away from St. Florian, and that is where he now lies, in the crypt below the great organ with which he cast a spell upon so many hearers.

It was at the organ that his timidity fell away from him; the caution we find in his early written music was not, we may be sure, to be found in his improvisations, and it is certainly significant that he wrote no organ music of any weight. The instrument became a function of himself, and he rarely wanted to play composed music on it, whether his own or others'; in his Upper Austrian dialect he is said to have remarked, "Let them as has no imagination play Bach and Mendelssohn —I'd rather let go on my own" (or so one might attempt to translate). There is a deep psychological reason for this, and it is naturally connected with his timorous attitude to composing itself. In the organ loft he was virtually unseen, and free; orchestras and choirs consisted of other people, and had to be written for—knowing he would have to commit his thoughts to them in permanent form he became, in a deep sense, shy, both of them and himself. He was also dimly aware of such people as smart intellectuals of the type who were later to make his life a misery in Vienna; encounters of this kind did nothing to improve his confidence. It took him many years to overcome this special personal difficulty (indeed, it may be said that he never quite conquered it), and the noble patience with which he learned to understand it is definitively expressed in nearly all his mature music.

One of the reasons for the legend about Bruckner's "sudden" flowering from mediocre talent into original genius is his astonishingly protracted assiduity in technical study. While studying counterpoint and theory with Simon Sechter between 1855 and 1861 (ages 31–37), he composed scarcely a note besides exercises; this was Sechter's strict rule, and Bruckner, docile and impressionable as always, concurred. One cannot help wondering if Sechter would have been as successful in thus fettering another composer who intended to study with him— Schubert! But Schubert was himself thirty when he decided to have these lessons, so Bruckner's late resolve was not without precedent. Not that Bruckner had by this time done anything remotely comparable with Schubert's miraculous achievement; but it is wrong to underestimate the quality of some of the music he wrote before the artistic celibacy imposed by his teacher. Simple and even primitive though some of it is, it is sometimes highly personal, and the first extended work, the D minor Requiem, is unmistakably by Bruckner. In 1849 he was appointed sub-organist at St. Florian. He was still undecided (in fact, until 1853) whether to become a musician or a civil servant, and it is not hard to imagine this odd little man leading a Bob Cratchit-like existence on a high stool. (It is perhaps more difficult to imagine a Cratchit composing Bruckner's Requiem.)

This work is austerely scored for solo voices, chorus, and an orchestra of three trombones, strings and (believe it or not in 1849) organ continuo, with the replacement of one of the trombones by a horn in the *Benedictus*. The very beginning, with its plain choral writing contrasted with mysteriously restless syncopations in the strings, is already characteristic. At this stage Bruckner knew little of Beethoven's orchestral music (he did not hear the Ninth Symphony until 1866), probably none of Schubert's, and it is doubtful if he was at all familiar with Haydn's or Mozart's, though it is likely that he was acquainted with the church music of the two latter masters, whose influence can be felt throughout his choral works, even near the end of his life. Haydn in particular may be discerned in the planning of all his masses with the exception of the E minor, and the Requiem has something of the simplicity and directness, as well as the severity, of some of Haydn's early and middle-period symphonies. There is a notable economy in the writing that throws finely into relief certain bold strokes, such as the placing of the polyphonic *Quam olim Abrahæ* in the impressively unexpected key of F minor, or the touching string of solos and choral responses accompanied by unpretentiously expressive string figuration in the *Agnus Dei*. Any musician looking at this score without knowing the composer would be bound to find it curiously individual, though he might well have difficulty in determining its period. For 1849 it seems archaic and provincial—but such objections are no more valid than the claims of the present-day *avant-gardiste* that anything not of next week must necessarily be outmoded. Choral societies of limited resources wanting an unusual work of no great technical difficulty

will find this little Requiem surprisingly rewarding and larger organiz-
ations could (as Hans-Hubert Schönzeler has suggested) pertinently
place it and Bruckner's Ninth Symphony in the same programme—
the beginning and the end of the real Bruckner. Certainly nothing
could be better calculated to dispel the idea that he wrote no valuable
and typical music before he was forty.

The next five years between 1849 and 1854 show a marked development in Bruckner's skill as a composer. He wrote a number of choral
pieces, large and small, with and without orchestra, most noteworthy a
Magnificat and Psalm 114, showing increasing fluency in handling
traditional techniques with flashes of personal insight, and culminating
in a full-scale mass, the *Missa solemnis* in B flat minor. There is nothing
mediocre or tentative about this strong and clear work; in some ways
it is a worthy and simpler successor to Haydn's masses, and it is curious
to contemplate the absence, as late as 1854, of any marked trace of even
Beethoven's or Schubert's influence. Taken on its own terms, however
(and we should never do otherwise with any composition), the music
is often of excellent quality. It is sometimes remarked that the opening
of the *Kyrie* anticipates that of the Ninth Symphony by its rise and fall
of a minor third, and it has been suggested that the theme in the
symphony (see Ex. 3 (a) on page 183) is a deliberate quotation of the
mass, but such conjectures are of no real importance beside the interest
of the B flat minor mass itself. We should inevitably be disappointed
if we expect this minor third to produce in the mass anything remotely
resembling the kind of music we find in the Ninth, but there is nothing
to prevent us enjoying the ease and, often, beauty of Bruckner's
classical invention in the early work; at the age of thirty he was already
an experienced and more than talented composer, with a natural gift
for counterpoint, a sympathy for voices, and an unobtrusive skill in
blending chorus and orchestra. In construction the work, though not
perfect, is admirable, and a study of it should provide an obvious lesson
to those who think Bruckner congenitally incapable of cogent designs.
He had learned plenty about the modes of progression and the forms of
classical music, and would have had no difficulty whatsoever in perfect-
ing this knowledge had he so chosen; one of the elementary things
we have to learn about him is the fact that all his later constructional
difficulties arise from his own originality, not from incompetence in
orthodox procedures. If his symphonic development had stuck to the
lines laid down cautiously but competently in the Overture in G minor
and the *Studiensymphonie* of 1863, he would no doubt have written

some excellent, blameless, and even powerful works, and would have been spared the disastrous mistakes of, say, the Third Symphony. But he had the courage to follow his own instinct with all the consequent tribulations and crises, artistic and personal.

The B flat minor mass was the last major work before the long period of abstinence under the stern eye of Sechter. This period is sometimes commented upon with amazement that any natural composer could so silence himself for so long. If one looks carefully at the music immediately preceding it—this mass and such things as the F minor *Libera* of the same year—it is easy to see how Bruckner could have been dissatisfied with his own growing facility. He was certainly not expecting his originality to be fostered by Sechter, but he needed a fallow period. Something must already have been stirring within him, though he scarcely knew what. He must have been more than vaguely aware that it was something significant, and his instinct told him that the only sure way to uncover it was to exorcise traditional habits by practising them to the point of exhaustion. It is probable that Sechter unknowingly brought out Bruckner's originality by insisting that it be suppressed until it could no longer be contained, and that Bruckner himself collaborated in this ruthless *régime* out of instinctive knowledge of what would eventually happen. We must not forget that his greatest psychological difficulty was in committing music to paper; in the organ loft he had no problems and, no doubt, improvising must have been a solace and an outlet for his creative urge during this time of nearly seven years. It must, in fact, have been a vital complement to his skull-cracking technical paper work; while he was laboriously mastering every conceivable aspect of theory, considering with painful thoroughness the very nature of the sounds of music, their constitutions and relationships, he must often have retired with relief to the organ keyboards, there to rediscover these sounds in new relationships. We may well wonder how many of the typically Brucknerian ideas of the later symphonies originated during this period.

At the end of this heroic labour Bruckner was examined at the Vienna *Konservatorium*, with the object of a diploma that would qualify him to teach harmony and counterpoint. Herbeck, one of the examiners (and afterwards one of Bruckner's most loyal friends), exclaimed "He should have examined us!" But Bruckner was still far from satisfied. Seeking instruction of a kind he could not get from Sechter, he took lessons in orchestration and orchestral composition from Otto Kitzler, and it was for him that he made his first symphonic essay, the F minor symphony of 1863, still deliberately curbing his own individuality. It is a well found piece of work, sometimes showing the influence of Schumann, as does Dvořák's C minor symphony of two years later, sometimes inclined to stiffness of movement, and somewhat less freely imaginative than the Overture in G minor that slightly preceded it. It is more than a mere exercise, though Bruckner never regarded it as anything else. The time of release was now close at hand. Kitzler had introduced him to the music of Liszt and Wagner and he became fascinated by its harmonic independence and the richness and power of Wagner's orchestration. At the end of his time with Sechter, Bruckner remarked that he felt like a watchdog that had snapped its chain; now he was ready to explore the fields.

The new expressive power of Bruckner's music is at once evident in the beginning of the D minor mass of 1864. He has not lost contact with the Haydn tradition, as the plan of the whole clearly shows, but the mysterious groping harmonies with which this work opens are all his own, and the mass as a totality has a fresh blunt strength. There are few moments of uncertainty anywhere in it, and its confident breadth and scope must have surprised anyone who knew only Bruckner's *gauche* exterior, but must only have confirmed the impressions of those who had heard him play the organ and who realized that at last he had found a way to put some of his grandest ideas (with which they had long been familiar) on to paper. The more we consider the supposed abrupt emergence of Bruckner as a creative genius, the clearer does it become that it was not lack of ideas that caused the delay, but difficulty in recording them. (It would be wonderful to have tape recordings of Bruckner's organ extemporizations; on the other hand, we should perhaps be thankful that such devices did not exist in his day, for he might never have bothered to write anything down.)

The Mass in D minor, with its trenchant choral writing and its certain treatment of the symphonic orchestra, its dramatic force and its frequent contemplative depth, was at that time the strongest of its kind since Beethoven, with the exception of Schubert's great Mass in A flat. It and Schubert's underrated masterpiece (a much finer work than his later Mass in E flat) are both equally neglected, and when we have given Schubert's work full recognition, we should turn our attention to Bruckner's D minor, which is overshadowed by the two masses that followed it in quick succession. The three mature masses of Bruckner occupied him between 1864 and 1868. All of them underwent a certain amount of revision, but not of the desperate kind that was subsequently suffered by some of the symphonies. The changes made in these choral scores were usually prompted by the composer's own practical experience of conducting performances, and not by the advice of the group of friends who wanted to "improve" the symphonies and who found him all too acquiescent to their views. Bruckner had more opportunities to conduct his church music than his symphonies; he was not a good conductor, but frequent contact with orchestras might have given him greater assurance in resisting the kind of pressures that caused him such trouble in later life. In the following chapters we shall examine, in such detail as is really necessary (but no more), the nature of these pressures in the revisions of individual symphonies, but the student of the masses will find with relief that there are few such snares for his judgment. Those in D minor and E minor, as well as the Linz version of the First Symphony, are evidence of a confidence that Bruckner was rarely to recapture. There is but one later period of the kind, the eight years from 1875 to 1883, during which the Fifth, Sixth and Seventh were composed, the least revised (by him) of all his mature symphonies.

For the past eight years before the composition of the D minor mass, Bruckner had been organist at Linz Cathedral. As we have noted, he had written almost nothing during this time, travelling regularly to Vienna to see Sechter. Now at the end of his Linz period came the three masses and the First Symphony, all of which were performed there with encouraging results. Of these four works, the two most remarkable are the Mass in E minor (No. 2) (1866) and the symphony. The latter will be analysed in the next chapter, and the mass would equally well bear close discussion. It is the most restrained and profound of the three, and has no soloists and an orchestra of wind only, and is the fruit of Bruckner's intense study of sixteenth-century polyphony. Its extended passages of *a cappella* writing and its comparatively austere harmony give it a much more strongly liturgical character than its companions, yet it is still essentially a concert work. The *Sanctus*, with its magnificent unaccompanied canonic growth to a climax, is based on a line from Palestrina; though it is hazardous and difficult in performance (the slightest loss of pitch means disaster when the brass enter), it is perhaps the finest single movement in the whole of Bruckner's early maturity. We can learn much from it by realizing that if he had conceived its idea in later life, he might well have treated it as an element in a vaster design; the opening of the Ninth Symphony is one such element, and comparing that with the *Sanctus* of the E minor mass can be of assistance in grasping the time-scale of the symphonies.

The terseness of such a work as the E minor mass should have a salutary effect on critics who find Bruckner's symphonies diffuse. Through such comparisons they may eventually come to appreciate the terseness with which he later treats passages as large as whole movements of the mass, the forms of which are simple but often subtle. Some are naturally dictated by the text, such as that of the *Kyrie*, opening with beautiful climbing harmonies that float over a tonic pedal and lead eventually to a more active middle section (*Christe eleison*); the whole movement should ideally be *a cappella*, for the wind parts are optional here, but it would be a first-rate choir that would take the risk of being corrected in pitch by the bassoons at the beginning of the *Gloria*. Other movements have finely organized structures independently of the text, for example the *Benedictus*, one of the most searchingly thoughtful parts of the mass, in a delicately poised sonata form, fully worked out. For succinct expressiveness, it would be difficult to surpass the melodic line of the *Crucifixus*, in which every single phrase is perfectly concentrated upon the meaning of its words, the whole forming an exquisitely balanced completed melody:

It is perhaps not often thought that Bruckner might have made a good song writer, but a passage like this makes one pause over such a possibility. There is no evidence that he showed much enjoyment of poetry, but when he sets words he is unfailingly observant and sensitive, whether or no there is any truth in the story of his reply to a poet who complained of word repetitions in one of his male voice pieces, "You didn't write enough words".

Not long after the completion of the Mass in E minor, Bruckner had a nervous breakdown. No doubt it was partly a delayed after-effect of his long-drawn period of unrelenting study, and it may also have been exacerbated by disappointment at his failures to obtain various posts in Salzburg and Vienna. But he was in any case prone to nervous disorders, from which he suffered all his life. After three months' rest and treatment at Bad Kreuzen, he was able to resume work, and began the third of the large masses, in F minor. It is possibly the most celebrated of the three, and is planned on a grand scale, expansive as the E minor is concentrated. Its composition occupied a year, September 1867 to September 1868. It makes use once more of the full symphony orchestra as well as solo voices and is the obvious successor to the D minor, which it exceeds in grandeur and spaciousness. It is not so profound as the E minor, though it is more immediately impressive. Its melodic invention is spontaneous and appealing, and it has many monumental passages, such as the splendid and original fugue on *In gloria Dei Patris*, or the wonderful treatment of *Et vitam venturi* with its indescribably grand punctuations of *Credo, credo* by the full-throated chorus. The orchestral writing, though it has not the striking individuality of that in the First Symphony, is beautifully calculated against the choir and the soloists, and contributes vitally to the expressive and dramatic moments in which the work abounds. Most musicians would probably say that this is the greatest of the masses, though I cannot escape a strong preference for the more subtle and intimate E minor, which I find more consistently deep. Comparing the two settings of the *Benedictus*, that in the E minor seems to me more penetrating than the extremely euphonious but slightly lush one in the F minor (which, incidentally, must have strongly influenced Mahler in the slow movement of his Fourth Symphony). But I would not willingly do without either work, for between them they show the remarkable range of expression of which Bruckner was capable in his field.

There is one other major work that properly belongs to the Linz period—the unnumbered D minor symphony that Bruckner subsequently christened *Die Nullte* (No. "o"). It must have been begun before the official No. 1, but was completed after it, in 1869. Bruckner was rather harsh in discarding it, for it is in many ways a fine work, but it is not hard to see why he did so. I suspect that the earliest part of it is the *Andante*, an often noble piece, but wanting in inner tension and a sense of climax; the Finale, too, may be partly of earlier origin, with its punctilious fugality and its slightly incongruous second theme (which, however, shows surprising energy in the recapitulation). The First Symphony is much more advanced than either of these movements, and its boldness received not a little harsh criticism when it was played (under Bruckner himself) in Linz in 1868. As always, he was disturbed by such strictures, and thought he had better produce something less aggressive next time. Although the facts are not certain, it seems likely that he returned to the *Andante* and *Finale* (and it may be that the *Scherzo*, too, is earlier than No. 1), revised them, and put them into a new symphony. Internal evidence suggests that the first movement of No. "o", at any rate, is later than any part of the First Symphony, for it shows distinctly the influence of Beethoven's Ninth, which Bruckner did not hear until 1866 when No. 1 was virtually finished. The manuscript of *Die Nullte* shows all the movements dated at different times in 1869, with the first movement definitely latest,* but it is of course possible that parts of the symphony may simply have been revised at that period. Whatever the facts, there can be no doubt of the remarkable quality of the first movement. The effect of Beethoven's Ninth on its opening and on the chromatic ground bass in its coda is obvious, but the piece as a whole has an utter originality of design and texture that plainly foreshadows the Bruckner to come. For all its individuality and force, the First stands very much alone among the symphonies; this movement, on the other hand, is the beginning of a gigantic process that was to produce a whole succession of typical works. It begins with one of those characteristic *nebulae* Bruckner became so fond of, and we find the definitive form of this one at the opening of No. 3. Here, however, the cloudy opening is used for its own sake, not as a background or preparation for a clear-cut theme or themes, and its figuration is itself the thematic source-material. When Bruckner showed the symphony to Otto Dessoff in Vienna (in the hope that he would perform it) his confidence was once more shattered by the blunt question "Where's the main theme?", and this may finally have caused him to discard the work.

But there are many things in this first movement that Bruckner should have been proud of—the fine purity and translucence of the scoring, the beauty and spontaneity of the melodic invention (if

* See Hans F. Redlich: *Bruckner's Forgotten Symphony "No. o"* (Music Survey, Vol. II, No. 1) (1949).

Dessoff could find no main theme, he could scarcely have complained about the wonderfully flowing and refined second group), and the perfectly realized, subtly calculated structure. The development, too, is unusual in growing for a long time from the simple cadence at the end of the exposition—not in any obvious way, but with cunningly oblique transformations of the material into seemingly new shapes that proliferate with total unpredictability, yet make a beautifully coherent and natural flow of ideas. At the beginning of the coda there is string writing of great originality, evocative of a fascinating atmosphere that Sibelius would have recognized. I can find no fault with this masterly piece of music.

The rest of the symphony is not on this level, but that is not to say that it is not worth hearing. If the slow movement lacks that organic growth and cumulative sense that has become so familiar in the mature Bruckner *adagio*, it also has some lovely things in it, notably the second theme, strangely Slavonic in character, as if it had dropped out of *Prince Igor* (I do not know how much Russian music Bruckner knew, but it is odd that this symphony is the only one of all his works to suggest its influence; the introduction to the Finale also has a curiously attractive Slav flavour). The Scherzo, on the other hand, suggests nothing so much as the influence of an enraged Rossini, with its vamping crotchets and its scurrying quavers that stop precipitately (in *fortissimo* the effect is as if the Barber had been punched on the nose by a dissatisfied customer). Yet it is still unmistakable though by no means mature Bruckner, with a hint of the weight to come in this part of later symphonies, while the Trio is totally original; though it is in G major, its beginning, coming after the D minor scherzo (which ends with a D major chord), sounds as if it is in D, with G major merely a subdominant. It is full of chromaticisms that keep the ear mystified until the end of the first part in D major, clearly meant to be a half close on the dominant, but sounding obstinately like a tonic. This may, for all I care, be a miscalculation, but it is so intriguing as to be a stroke of genius, and the return of the theme at bar 37 is contrived with such breathtaking naïvety as to constitute a miracle. One could nearly laugh out loud at the inspired *gaucherie* of it, while being much moved by the poetry behind it. The Finale has a slow introduction that recurs before the development, and its Russian-ecclesiastical atmosphere leads into aggressively solemn (at times academic) contra-puntal junketings, *Allegro vivace*, during which Bruckner is not likely to be offended if we fail to keep a straight face. The second subject is like something too unwieldy for Schubert to have been able to cram into one of his Italian overtures (in the restatement Bruckner is very unkind to the cellos). The development investigates the contrapuntal possibilities of the main theme with much dust and smoke, and in the recapitulation the elephantine ballerina of a second subject unexpectedly thunders into a splendidly stormy coda. It is altogether a cumbrously diverting piece. The symphony as a whole does not deserve its neglect; all of it is enjoyable, and the first movement is a masterpiece.

From now on Bruckner's chief interest was to be the symphony; from time to time he wrote small choral works, but no more masses, and it was not until the *Te Deum* of 1881 that he returned to music for soloists, chorus, and orchestra. Some commentators have suggested that the reason for this was that Bruckner's new conception of the symphony was as a kind of substitute for or derivative of the mass; this idea is, I think, a little facile. It is true that the apparently sectional nature of some of Bruckner's larger symphonic movements could easily enough be interpreted as reflecting the changes of character and pace in some wordless *Gloria* or *Credo*, but this view would not only take too narrow a view of the range of expression encompassed in the symphonies, but would also ignore fundamental musical and structural differences between the two kinds of work. I do not intend this objection in a generalized sense (i.e. that for any composer the problems of composing a mass are basically different from those involved in a symphony, though that is also true), but with particular reference to Bruckner's own artistic development. When he turned from composing masses to symphonies it was because he began to evolve a new type of musical motion. All his work up to 1868, both ante- and post-Sechter, was firmly in the classical tradition, with one solitary exception, the Mass in E minor. Although this was composed in 1866, before Bruckner had come under the influence of Kitzler's enthusiasm for Wagner, it already shows an incipient new sense of slow movement, ostensibly derived from the comparatively static music of the sixteenth century, but in reality adumbrating something else. We have already noticed that the *Sanctus* of this work is like the kind of vast *crescendo* process which Bruckner was able later to absorb into a larger whole; typical examples would be the openings of the Finale of the Fourth Symphony and the first movement of the Ninth, and the codas of most of his mature first and last movements. This type of composition is radically opposed to the athletic treatment of tonality and innate dramatic fluidity of the classical sonata-symphony, and is also basically against the kind of music Bruckner himself was composing. The masses in B flat minor, D minor, and F minor show a steady advance in mastery of the type of mass already made familiar by Haydn, Mozart, Beethoven and Schubert, a type far more closely allied to the classical symphony than are Bruckner's symphonies to his own tradition-based masses. Any one of these three masses will show, almost at a glance, that its sense of movement is classical, and it does not take much more than a glance to show that the E minor is fundamentally different. The E minor is often construed as a deliberately archaic, retrospective work, Bruckner's tribute to Palestrina and Company, but it is really the first hint of the later composer. While its *Gloria* and *Credo* retain a contact with the world of classical music, its *Kyrie*, *Sanctus*, and *Agnus Dei* pay lip-service to an older world while entering a new one, and the subtle *Benedictus* holds a fine balance. So far forward does the *Sanctus* look that not only does it foreshadow later processes by Bruckner himself, but we can also find something very like it in Sibelius's Seventh Symphony. For many years I was under the delusion that the E minor was really the last of Bruckner's masses and that the numbering had somehow gone wrong. The facts seem to refute this, but I shall never be surprised if someone finally proves them to be otherwise.

The next influence to impinge on Bruckner was Wagner's. This, too, stirred something instinctive in him. It did not greatly affect (certainly not very much at first) the colouring of his music or the shape of its themes, but Bruckner felt at once the enormous and unprecedented slowness of Wagner's processes. These were aimed at creating musical designs large enough to embrace whole acts of stage dramas. Bruckner's interest in the stage proceedings was minimal (he is reputed to have asked, at the end of *Die Walküre*, why they had set fire to Brünnhilde), but the majestic deliberation of Wagner's invention and its growth into vast forms fascinated him. Inevitably we find him picking up Wagnerian touches of harmony or instrumentation, and occasionally a typical *gruppetto* or *appoggiatura* will betray its origin. But Bruckner was probably the first composer to be successful in transferring this kind of slowness to pure instrumental music, at least as a pervasive principle. In Beethoven we can find almost everything (the slow movement of the *Hammerklavier* sonata is as slow as anything in Wagner, and that of the A minor quartet dwarfs the achievement of Bruckner's E minor mass in the way it blends radically opposed currents), but in no composer earlier than Bruckner can we discover a consistent exploration of the problem. It became his life's work, leading him to the invention (or, rather, evolution) of new forms, to occasional disaster but also to the creation of a type of symphonic finale that, when it is successful, is unique. In his hands the symphony developed peculiar new characteristics that no one hitherto has successfully imitated. It can be argued, of course, that as the Haydn or Beethoven mass is derived from the classical symphony, so Bruckner evolves a new type of symphony from the classical mass, but this is to omit the vital factor of a kind of movement inimical to such a theory and to obscure the fact that Bruckner's symphonies, far from being instrumental corollaries to his masses, are a decisive break with the tradition they represent.

This chapter is not the place to summarize the nature of the Bruckner symphony. As we shall find out in the ensuing analyses, generalizations of that sort are apt to be misleading, for the symphonies separately attempt or achieve different solutions to the common problem of how to create coherent instrumental forms on such a time-scale. But it is as well to note in advance that the problem was not solved all at once. The First Symphony does not tackle it, for Bruckner had not yet cut free from classical tradition; no doubt he himself would have explained the E minor mass of the same year purely as a glance back to an even older tradition. Nor does *Die Nullte* break away; it shows the tremendous effect the opening of Beethoven's Ninth Symphony must have had on his imagination, and it proceeds on lines that, though they are highly individual (at times to the point of idiosyncrasy), distribute and convey tensions of basically familiar kind. But there is in the first movement of this symphony a calm spaciousness that breathes a new atmosphere. Bruckner is already scenting the air of new country through an open window, out of which he will soon attempt perilously to climb. The descent is hazardous, but he makes a promising exit with the last movement of No. 2, without realizing how far it is to the ground, and swings crazily on the rope in No. 3. In the Finale of the Fourth he slips again, not quite so dizzily, for he is nearer *terra firma*, which he triumphantly treads in the Fifth. After this, such errors as he makes are no longer dangerous, though the country is not always an Arcadia, to judge from his strange findings in the Finale of No. 6, or the profound disturbances of No. 8, or the final agonies so poignantly expressed in parts of No. 9.

Bruckner's slow processes have often led to misunderstandings, especially on the part of those who persist in associating his symmetries

with those of sonata. Such critics are diminishing in number, but there
are still enough to make it necessary to deal with the point. Mis-
interpretation of these symmetries can lead to expectation of the tensions of sonata and disappointment at their absence, or their appearance
in seemingly wrong places. A true sonata movement creates certain
symmetries, but it is a grave mistake to suppose that the presence of
roughly similar symmetries indicates an attempt at sonata structure.
In a genuine sonata movement of even the quietest kind the moment
of *reprise*, for instance, is a dramatic incident depending on a special
kind of tension, expressed through a fundamentally dynamic sense of
key. Bruckner always possessed this sense, demonstrated in successful
sonata movements, and on such occasions produces the right kind of
tonal tension at the right moments. It is such tensions—not the presence
of expository or recapitulatory symmetries—that define the nature of
sonata. There are plenty of sonata movements without regular or even
obvious recapitulations, and plenty of other types of music that
recapitulate. All large-scale musical designs need to create some sense
of symmetry, or balance, if they are to satisfy a normal listener's
instinct for unity. This is true even of so fluid a music as fugue, where
the *dénouement* is properly produced at a strategic moment when the
listener's desire for symmetry has been stretched to breaking point.
In the great harmonic forms, of which sonata is the most influential,
symmetry tends to reveal itself in more broadly recognizable ways.
It is thus easily assumed that because sonata is so common it is automatically indicated by the presence of such symmetry. But birds and
bats, whatever the cursory glance may suggest, are unrelated. Most
extended structures that are harmonically based will tend to recapitulate sooner or later; there will also be transitional moments and often
we will know when the end is in sight—we are then listening to a
coda. The opening of any piece of thematic music will have either an
introductory or an expository feeling about it. If, however, we insist
on relating all these elements in Bruckner to sonata form, regardless of
their internal functions, we have only ourselves to blame for the
consequences of using our eyes rather than our ears.

It is such matters as these we shall encounter in detail in the following
chapters. In the meantime there remain three works that cannot be
left out of this preliminary survey, the String Quintet and the two late
choral works, the *Te Deum* of 1881 and Psalm 150, composed in 1892.
Apart from motets and part-songs (some of which are striking and
original, and I would strongly recommend *Abendzauber*, for baritone,

male voices, and four horns, a ravishing piece written in 1878 and breathing the same atmosphere as the opening of the Fourth Symphony) Bruckner wrote in the rest of his life only these three works and symphonies. In cold print this may not seem much, but in truth he had set himself a gigantic task, and the fact that he cannot have fully explained it to himself made it all the more difficult, fraught with error and gropings. The mighty achievement of the Fifth Symphony, despite adverse personal circumstances, must have given him greater confidence, and it is not without significance that this and the two symphonies that followed it received less revision than any others. The Fifth is a work of magnificently severe and massive consistency, and it must have been a strange task for Bruckner to follow such music with a string quintet, requested by Joseph Hellmesberger, who really wanted a quartet to play. Bruckner insisted that he preferred the richer possibilities of a quintet; he had soon after his time with Sechter attempted a quartet, a dry and tentative affair. Chamber music had never much attracted him and he approached this proposition with some diffidence, though not so much hesitation as Hellmesberger displayed when he saw the finished result—he refused to play it, even after some revisions had been made, and it was eventually performed by another ensemble, in which Franz Schalk played the second viola.

The Quintet has many beauties and it is only at the ends of the first and last movements that Bruckner's need for the orchestra reveals itself. The *Adagio* is one of his finest, indeed one of the most inspired things in chamber music since the last quartets of Beethoven; although it is fully on the scale of his symphonic slow movements, it never oversteps the limits of the medium. It contains two of the most beautiful themes Bruckner ever wrote, the first of truly Beethovenian serenity and the second unsurpassed for sheer purity and warmth of expression, even by Schubert, whose spirit it finely recaptures. The first movement is subtle in feeling, texture and structure, and the frequent wide leaping of its counterpoint, coupled with unexpected chromatic inflexions, creates a world of sound that is quite new. The Scherzo (which is placed second) is one of his most endearingly grotesque inspirations; moderate in pace, and also full of strange leaps and quirks of harmony and tonality, it wears an oddly dishevelled air, for all the world as if it were a self-portrait of the awkward nonplussed figure of the composer, trying to appear unconcerned though he knows he looks hopelessly out of place in sophisticated Vienna. It was this piece that was too much for Hellmesberger, who afterwards persuaded

Bruckner to substitute a comparatively suave *Intermezzo*; but this did not oust the original so much more characterful Scherzo. Only the Finale of the Quintet is not fully satisfactory as a piece of composition (the first movement's ending is a little ludicrously orchestral, but it can be lived down). Here Bruckner is still absorbed in the problem of the symphonic finale of his own peculiar stamp, and forgets that the tonal scale of five string instruments is unsuitable for such architecture. At least, he forgets it some of the time, and that is enough to create confusion. He starts as if to make introductory signals, to set the scene for the kind of basically contemplative process we find in one of his typical symphonic finales, sees that he cannot accumulate sufficient decisive invention to make the beginning sound like a real beginning, and lands himself with the curious sensation of seeming to start with his "second subject" (see bar 33). The "main" theme is never more than a token gesture and always seems either introductory or transitional; it is the second theme and its offshoots that have to do all the work, including some original but rather forced contrapuntal labour in the development. Even so, this movement has much in it that can be enjoyed and the Quintet as a whole is one of the treasures of nineteenth-century chamber music. The *Adagio* is of uncorrupted sublimity. The experience of the Quintet must certainly have had an effect on the Sixth Symphony, where there is a new refinement of orchestral sound, especially in the string department.

Bruckner's last two choral works are interesting to compare with the masses of the 1860s. The first thing that strikes one is that there is much less difference between, say, the F minor mass and the *Te Deum* than there is between the First and Seventh symphonies (to take roughly contemporaneous instances). Such a situation is inevitable after so long a neglect of large-scale choral music and so intense a concentration on orchestral. The second noticeable thing is that both the *Te Deum* and Psalm 150 are compact works; Bruckner does not show any inclination to produce a choral masterpiece in the time-scale of the symphonies. The sense of movement in these works is classical, though sometimes in the *Te Deum* we encounter the impressively ejaculatory manner of delivering ideas in *quanta* that sometimes occurs in the symphonic finales. The *non confundar* of the *Te Deum* makes use of an idea which became Ex. 6 in the Seventh Symphony soon afterwards (see p. 149). The symphony reveals the natural time-scale of the idea, which creates a slight sense of congestion in the confines of the *Te Deum*, resulting in a trace of embarrassment in the slightly contrived ending, with its rather commonplace fanfares. This is the only flaw in a masterful work of almost barbaric grandeur. Psalm 150 is even finer, and here there is no sign of confusion of time-scales. Even more compact than the *Te Deum*, it drives with unerring force to a great climax of the utmost simplicity and power.

Having made a rough survey of Bruckner's path, we must now go back and examine in detail the landmarks we have so far but glanced at. The nine numbered symphonies which embody the real development of Bruckner must necessarily dominate this book. Much more could be written about the masses, the Quintet, and the two late choral pieces, and we have said almost nothing of the many interesting smaller things. But this essay is aimed toward the understanding of Bruckner's musical mentality, and is not meant to be an annotated catalogue. The symphonies absorbed the whole of his specially characteristic evolution, and it is they that have been most often misunderstood. Anyone who can enjoy a Haydn mass should have little trouble with one by Bruckner, but not everyone who values Haydn's symphonies is able to relish Bruckner's. So it is on them we must now turn our attention.

CHAPTER II

SYMPHONY NO. 1, IN C MINOR

THERE ARE TWO authentic versions of the official No. 1. The original score dates from 1865/6 (Linz) and the later revision, by Bruckner himself, was carried out in 1890/1 (Vienna). There are no fundamental changes in the structure; the basic shape remains the same in the revision, odd bars being dropped or added here and there. But there is a great deal of re-working over details, both in scoring and in the substance of the music itself, and passages are actually re-composed. The Vienna score is rarely an improvement over the original, and often the simplicity and urgency of Bruckner's inspiration in Linz is ruined by fussy and frequently difficult detail. The revision betrays the composer's nervousness and perhaps his state of health. Things were not going well for him—he had not recovered from the shock of Hermann Levi's rejection of the Eighth in its original form, and was painfully wrestling with the Ninth. His friends were constantly suggesting (or actually making) revisions in his earlier works, and he became possessed of a somewhat desperate revising mania. Of the revisions he is known to have made himself, that of the First Symphony is the worst. Yet it is a document of deep interest, if only because it reveals the disturbed condition of Bruckner's mind at the time. The calm clear basses of the original are frequently made restive, and decorative figurations that were beautiful and simple in the earlier score were often rendered tortuous (for a typical example compare letter J, first movement, in the revision, with letter E in the original). Scoring, though more varied, sometimes was coarsened; there is a peculiarly horrible instance in the final climax of the *Adagio* (letter G in both scores), and disruptively nervy tempo fluctuations were added (with especial damage to the Finale). Compared with this, Schumann's panicky re-scoring of his D minor symphony was harmless. It is true that the Vienna version of Bruckner's First contains refinements and subtleties that the composer of the Linz version would not have thought of, but most of them are of a kind that could have been apt only in his later works. If we want to know what the symphony is really like we must turn to its bold, clean Linz version, and it is unlikely that its bluntness will now strike us (as it must have done the agitated old man of the 1890s) as crudeness. Such impurities as it has are less disturbing than the anachronisms that were afterwards imposed upon it.

The dogged opening of this symphony is not characteristic of the mysterious breadth we have come to expect of a Bruckner beginning. Tramping crotchets become background to a glum march-theme pervaded by dotted rhythms. It is noteworthy that the start of the next symphony (the so-called "No. 0", in D minor) also produces a tramping background—not to a theme, however, but to the kind of orchestral nebula that itself became the normal Brucknerian opening. (This fact alone would indicate that the opening of the D minor symphony was written after, not before, No. 1). Notice how the main theme, at first ambiguously suggesting A flat tonality, stretches itself, then tightens its muscles again as it rises to the brief *tutti* that crashes in upon a chord of A flat major. This composer is neither inexperienced nor amateurish:

Ex 1 (Vln 1)

When the theme resumes quietly (bar 28)* the marching crotchets underneath it are solidly in A flat. Yet the sense of C minor as the main key is unmistakable, established by hint rather than assertion; Bruckner has a subtle and original way with tonality that is altogether unbumpkinlike. Make a mental note, too, of the fact that the plain repeated chords of the start have now become thematic, derived from the string figuration in the previous *tutti* (Ex. 1 (d)):

Ex 2 (bar 28)

The march rhythms vanish, and wind instruments muse upon the figure of Ex. 1 (d), making a gentle transition towards E flat, open and clear after the tonal mystifications of the beginning, and we discover an arching *cantabile*; it is perhaps surprising to find how often Bruckner is content with two-part writing:

Ex. 3 (bar 45)

The *tutti* to which this leads is based mostly on Ex. 1 (d) combined with a new woodwind figure of which (b) becomes the definitive shape:

Ex 4 (bar 67)

* Bar numbers and rehearsal letters refer to the Linz score, except where otherwise stated.

In the revision Bruckner altered this figure and put it on the horns. So far the music has been behaving in a classical manner—somewhat rough-hewn perhaps, but not disconcertingly so. Everything has been close-knit, and this *tutti* suggests that the exposition will soon come to a vigorous end, the first stage in a movement that is likely to be short. But the music begins to broaden unexpectedly. Is the *tutti* going to sweep over into the development? There are certainly signs of modulation, as alien harmony invades the scene. The excitement increases. Then comes an immense surprise. A massive new theme, majestic on the trombones, strides suddenly into view. It is in E flat, and in slower tempo (*Mit vollster Kraft, im Tempo etwas verzögernd*), with a sweeping Tannhäuser-like accompaniment rising and falling in waves:

The accompaniment loses all its thrilling inevitability in the revision, and it is a mystery how Bruckner could have brought himself to substitute such fussy fiddlings for so magnificently simple a conception.* Be that as it may, this passage has no precedent or successor in symphonic music and, when it subsides, E flat major is once more in control. A soft cadential phrase ends the exposition:

Bruckner confirms this by drawing a double bar-line. The slower pace continues. The prospects of the movement are immeasurably extended. The quiet music based on Ex. 6 goes on for a while, moving away from E flat. It is softly disturbed by a suggestion of the sweeping accompaniment figure from the previous passage, and then the *tutti* breaks out again, subsiding after five bars into harmony that drifts towards C flat. In the meantime Ex. 6 (a) (which is a transformation of Ex. 5 (a)) extends its last two notes plaintively:

* It is possible that he felt the original was too much like the figurations of Tannhäuser, but its effect is quite different.

Ex 7 (bar 127)

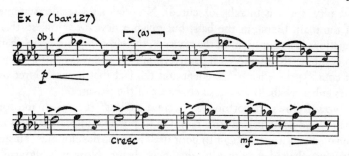

The harmony brightens into the dominant of G major (bar 142). But all the while the two notes of Ex. 7 (a) are beginning to sound vaguely familiar, and the entry of the first theme of all (Ex. 1), by now almost forgotten, is confirmation that Ex. 7 (a)—and in retrospect Ex. 5 (a)—is really Ex. 1 (c). At this point F sharp minor contradicts the expected G major and by doing so makes a dramatic point of the whole incident. This is subtlety, both thematic and tonal, of an order that should make all but the most obtuse of Bruckner's detractors think twice about condescending to him. The subtlety is consummated by the fact that the *appoggiatura* Ex. 1 (c)-cum-5 (b)-cum-7 (a), having done its job in suggesting the main theme, modestly retires from the scene, at least for the time being.

The return of the rhythm of Ex. 1 naturally enlivens the tempo, and after a little dalliance with a new but short-lived figure (horn, bar 144), the original speed is resumed (Tempo 1, bar 156), and a full-scale development of the *Allegro* material ensues, with powerful and abrupt dynamic contrasts. It swings round to the home dominant at bar 193, in hushed expectancy of the recapitulation. In a movement unmistakably in C minor, this is (except for one solitary bar, 16) the first use of the home dominant, three-quarters of the way through! And if we look at bar 16, we see that there the home dominant is at once contradicted. Here, for the first time in the movement, it is confirmed. Bruckner is no model for students, but we can all learn from him. In the Linz score, incidentally, the tonic confirmation is finely anticipated by a *pianissimo* kettledrum, a detail with which the old man seems to have been impatient in Vienna.

The theme moves, as before, to the *tutti* beginning on an A flat chord. This time the harmony turns to the sharp side, very softly corrected by the drum on C (bar 223) (its entry is delayed in the revision so that it coincides with the change from strings to woodwind

B

—a pity, for it is thereby obscured). Now comes a counterstatement of the main theme in the bass, but given a new direction, so that it functions as a transition. In the revision, the old composer sees a chance to combine the theme with its inversion (one of his favourite devices, of course); the effect is excellent and the fact that it ceases after four bars enhances the transitional character of the passage.

Now follows the orthodox "second subject" (Ex. 3) in the tonic major, and again it leads to a *tutti*. On its previous appearance this *tutti* behaved as if it were about to pour itself into the development; instead Bruckner halted it with a mighty new theme. Now it is allowed its head as it surges into a *coda* in which the string figuration of Ex. 1 (d) takes many new forms, developed by a fascinating and spontaneous process of gradual change. Throughout the *coda* the *allegro* is sustained (except for two dramatic pauses) and Ex. 5 does not return. There is no need to recapitulate a surprise which now stuns by its absence. A proper romantic composer would have used it to crown the movement (or even the whole symphony) with ponderous rhodomontade, but Bruckner justly makes it the more impressive in retrospect, at the heart rather than the end of the piece, preferring to close with severely trenchant formal matter. The Linz version is of great purity in this respect, but Bruckner's revision of the *coda* is, in one place at least, disastrous. Ex. 3, which has perfectly served its purpose as a lyrical contrast whose thematic separateness is itself a complete function, is dragged in *fortissimo* on the trumpet (letter X, Universal Edition) like a brazen harlot! Was it really Bruckner who perpetrated this red-hot horror?

Originality is certainly one of the most notable attributes of the first movement, but the *Adagio* surpasses it in this respect as well as in depth. Like so many aspects of Bruckner, his slow movements are uniquely characteristic, but we should beware of generalizing too easily about them. Precisely because he is such an original, even idio-syncratic composer, there is a tendency to make "global" statements about his music. In fact there are only a few things that are invariable in his work. These are no more than fingerprints, heavy ones, it is true, but not essentially any more important than the obviously recognizable habits of a striking personality. Sometimes they lead to weaknesses, as can all mannerisms when they become too automatic— the use of sequence, inversion, simple regularity of phrase-length, they all can become liabilities when Bruckner nods. Yet his attention fails infrequently, and anxiety to leave no tone unturned (if I may avoid a *cliché*) is much more likely to be a source of trouble.* But so far as form is concerned, no two movements of this composer closely resemble each other, and he rarely makes a move without a purpose suited only to the matter in hand. Sometimes we have to listen very carefully for his purpose before we can understand that something is going on that is very different from the chance semblances of established forms our habits have led us to assume. Even the deepest and most observant of musical minds, such as Tovey's, can be caught out. As we proceed to examine the slow movements of Bruckner's symphonies in the course of this book, we cannot do better than test against each one of them Tovey's description—"The plan of his *adagios* consists of a broad main theme, and an episode that occurs twice, each return of the main theme displaying more movement in the accompaniment and rising at the last return to a grand climax, followed by a solemn and pathetic die-away *coda*". This, of course, is not based on an assumption connected with forms established outside Bruckner's work, but it is, as we shall see, a rash generalization.

The very opening of the *Adagio* of No. 1 already dispels any idea of a "broad main theme". Like the beginning of the first movement, it shows tonal ambiguity—but much more markedly, and it anticipates the *Adagio* of the Ninth Symphony in the way it seems to be searching for a key. Dark gropings around the region of F minor climb towards the light, sink again, make another attempt. Here is the gloomy, fragmentary start, rising to the first outcry, whence it falls:

Ex 8
Adagio

* Bruckner was not addicted to retrograde inversions; fortunately for himself he left for another generation the nightmarish worry of how to leave no tone unsterned.

After the second cry (bar 16) there comes a consolatory phrase, like a calm chorale. It is in a clear A flat major, and this is the tonic the music has been seeking:

Ex 9 (bar 18)

The air has cleared, and Bruckner moves with a quiet deliberation until he arrives at a chord of B flat major (bar 30). Above a flowing accompaniment appears a fine curving melody:

Ex 10 (bar 30)

B flat is treated as if it were a key, and the melody is joined by gracious counterpoints. But B flat is not here a key—it proves to be the dominant of E flat, and in E flat the melody alights, reaching a broad climax in a remarkably short time. The device of simultaneously shortening and broadening a design by allowing the second group to commence while the transition is still in progress is perhaps derived from Schubert, another master whose subtleties have sometimes been misconstrued as faults by the unwary. Bruckner is careful to avoid a direct full close (the only root chord of E flat in this section is half-way through bar 41) and the actual end of the passage is a preparation for the next (bar 43). Although the very slow tempo has absorbed a considerable time so far, the musical process from the beginning of the movement has been very concise. There are surprisingly few notes to be actually counted, and no composer could have been more economical. Now is the time to relax the mental tension.

The key of E flat remains as, with a change to three-four time, a new idea flows quietly in. It is a *cantabile* of great beauty, in some ways prophetic of the famous *Moderato* in the slow movement of the Seventh Symphony, easeful and noble:

Ex 11 (bar 44)

This beautiful *aria* shows signs of becoming a regular ternary form in itself (the oboe entry at bar 60 has all the sense of beginning a middle section) but instead it expands calmly through changing shades of harmony and colour until its semiquavers begin to flow continuously. The tranquillity is overcast. The flowing violin line becomes mysterious, masking the return of the dark elements. The semiquavers persist, to add power to the recapitulation—so there is here at least a half-truth in "each return of the main theme displaying more movement in the accompaniment". But in this case there is no broad main theme in the usual sense of the term, and the matter that fills its place returns but once. Bruckner writes a wonderful new transition to Ex. 10 (see bars 135–40), which is rescored and has its climax extended as it passes from E flat to A flat (corresponding to its original move from B flat to E flat). In revising this climax Bruckner was clearly afraid that the melodic lines in the strings would be swamped by the brass. His solution is coarse and ugly, merely underlining a slight weakness of melodic invention at this point (letter G in both scores), and the purer sound of the original is far preferable, even if the conductor must take care in balancing it. After the climax there is a serene *coda* upon which no trace of the earlier unquiet is permitted to creep, and A flat major rests itself.

The design of the *Adagio* is thus an unusual blend of ternary and sonata forms, a sonata exposition followed by a middle section based on new material (Ex. 11)—not a development, but the first stage of a ternary structure that changes its nature, drifting into the sonata recapitulation instead of returning to a formal one of its own. It would be easy but wrong to call Ex. 11 the final theme of the exposition, initiating the development; considered from the point of view of normal classical sonata, this "development" would seem to lack momentum. As soon as one realizes that it is no development at all, but the very opposite until it begins to behave *as if it had been a development*, the full subtlety of Bruckner's idea is manifest. In order to escape the pitfalls of faulting Bruckner with misunderstanding sonata "style", we must ourselves be sure that we understand it. In the case of this movement, misapprehension of this point is not fatal, but it can be in some later instances, especially the first movement of the Seventh Symphony and some of the finales.

Bruckner has often been accused of being a slave to the four-bar period. The charge is not without justice, but it is by no means so comprehensive as is usually supposed. We must, moreover, be wary of levelling such a criticism at him whenever we find four-bar phrases for long stretches at a time. Very frequently this kind of regularity is a source of power. Such a piece, for example, as the mighty Scherzo of the Eighth would be ruined by interruption of the regularity with anything but the occasional phrase of six bars. But there are cases when uniformity of this kind causes stagnation, and these we shall mention in their place. Meanwhile it must be observed that Bruckner uses irregular phrasing far more often than is generally realized, especially in his earlier works, while as late as the Finale of the Fifth Symphony we find such freedom, achieved with great mastery and plasticity, as Brahms would have been forced to admire if he could have been persuaded to take a really good look at the music. The Scherzo of No. 1 begins with the following series of bar-periods before it settles down into clearly recognizable groups of four—7, 2, 4, 2, 6, 4, 6. The effect is completely natural; the ear is intrigued, and then satisfied when the regularity appears. In its weight and bluntness this movement is already a characteristic Bruckner scherzo, and is based on two elements, the arpeggiated figures at the beginning, and this simple theme, from which the last three notes tend to detach themselves:

Ex 12 (bar 9)

The key is G minor, rather startling after the A flat of the *Adagio*, and a key that has hardly been touched upon in the previous two movements, neighbour though it is of C minor. Bruckner is always sensitive to such effects, and the avoidance of a tonality with a view to its ultimate emergence much later in a work can produce marvellous results in, for instance, the Seventh and Eighth symphonies (it must be stressed that the magic of the device is effective whether or not the listener understands why). This scherzo is in the classical cast with two halves (or a third and two-thirds) the first ending on the dominant, and both repeated, though the composer removed the second repeat in the revision. The passage immediately following the double bar consists mainly of accumulative repetition of Ex. 12 (a) in combination with the *arpeggio* figures, while the tonality swings back to G minor for a return of the opening. These repetitions become a little automatic, causing a drop rather than a rise in tension.

The Trio is an exquisitely original inspiration, in G major, totally unpredictable, beautifully instrumented and with some lovely harmonic shifts. Bruckner in the role of miniaturist is not a familiar figure, perhaps, but this and the trios of the Fourth and Fifth symphonies show how delicately aphoristic he could be.

The revision changes a few details, not always for the better, and adds a short link to the Scherzo *reprise*, which follows directly with Ex. 12, instead of returning to the *fortissimo* opening as in the original. The straightforward formality of the earlier procedure is somehow preferable in its directness. In both versions the Scherzo is finally extended into a forcible *coda*, slightly broadened, with advantage, in the revision.

Unlike most of Bruckner's finales, that of the First Symphony is a real *allegro*. It is also the only one of his larger symphonic movements that starts *fortissimo*, and Bruckner later found its abruptness comic, suggesting it was like a man bursting unexpectedly through a door— *Da bin i!* (Here I am!). He damped down the brass and drums in the revision, but spoilt the effect of what is by no means comic—a powerfully energetic and impressive opening. It is this movement that suffers most in the revision, through ruinous changes of tempo, meddlesome tinkerings with the scoring, and the occasional addition or subtraction of bars to make irregular periods uniform. The original is in almost every respect vastly superior, and where passages were later recomposed the clarity and directness of the Linz score is often reduced to a painful shambling. Compare the two versions of the *fugato* (Linz, letter G, Vienna, bar 212): the alterations not only make much of the counterpoint ugly and forced, they compel Bruckner into a regrettable slowing of the tempo in order to make them playable with reasonable intelligibility. All this is symptomatic of the neurotic condition of the composer in the last few years, and although some of the changes he made are good, he had clearly lost contact with the feelings that generated the original and was controlled by irrelevant ideas. If Bruckner himself could so spoil his own work, how wary we should be of the attempts of others to improve it!

The unspoilt Finale has irresistible impetus. There are one or two passages of slightly academic "business", but the energy is strongly sustained. The fierce start throws out a figure whose rhythm is more important than its melodic shape:

Its second bar soon becomes diminished (woodwind, bar 9), and the new quicker rhythm, with a lively string accompaniment, gathers itself together for a *crescendo* and a counterstatement of the opening. Again the volume subsides quickly and the music turns away from C minor, settling in E flat major with a new theme so full of character that it is difficult to get it out of one's head:

The Linz version approaches this idea by way of a three-bar phrase that makes the start of the theme seem delightfully eager, and it is typical of the revision that it squares the phrase-rhythms at this point. The woodwind take up Ex. 15 and a *tutti* confirms E flat, at first rather stiffly but with increasing freedom as the rushing semiquavers of the strings and interjections of the brass become less predictable. The revised version destroys this effect by bringing in the rhythm of Ex. 14, so pervasive in much of the movement that some relief from it is desirable, particularly in fully-scored passages where it is too easily expected. During this *tutti* (in both versions) one of the string figurations becomes important:

Ex 16 (bar 58)

The *fortissimo* stops dramatically with Ex. 16 (b). Then in only eight bars the four-note figure, now in quiet crotchets, makes a new cadential theme and a full close in E flat. It contains a reference to Ex. 14 (b):

Ex 17 (bar 83)

This ends the exposition and, as in the first movement, Bruckner punctiliously draws a double bar-line. Reminding us of Ex. 14, the last bar of Ex. 17 brings back the whole of the opening rhythm, now shaped anew:

Ex. 18 (bar 88)

For a time the mood is reflective, as always at this stage in a Bruckner finale, whether sonata principles are operative or not. Then the music begins to march more purposefully as Ex. 18 is subjected to the inevitable inversion, with a *pizzicato* accompaniment. The tonality moves as far away from E flat as possible, in the direction of A minor and major, and horns and trombones restore the erect version of Ex. 18, *fortissimo*, the strings taking up the bow in *staccato* quavers. A big *tutti* develops in which the phrasing becomes fascinatingly ambiguous; between bars 120 and 130 a situation arises that is by no means uncommon in the earlier Bruckner. First, a straightforward four-bar phrase (120–3) is put out by the brass. They begin what seems like another (124), but in bar 125 the woodwind start a new thought (oddly like the main theme of the last movement of Dvořák's "New World" Symphony). The trumpets, however, have a certain loyalty to their colleagues the horns and trombones, and although they find themselves entering with the woodwind, they stop when they realize that the four-bar phrase of the brass is due to finish, even though their friends, obviously put off, have given up the ghost a bar early. Not to be outdone, the woodwind add another bar to make theirs a five-bar phrase. The total result is a richly active six-bar period (124-9). With the exception of the violas (who will always tell you they are the most intelligent string players, and who have seized on a new rhythm at bar 125), the strings have all this time been solidly working away at quavers. At bar 130 the violas' rhythm becomes the means of heaving everything back to the normality of four-bar phrasing. All this description may seem like making a mountain out of a molehill, but it is necessary if only because Bruckner's phrasing is so often criticized by people who look no farther than the surface, or who accept old wives' tales without question. Bruckner is frequently subtle in this matter, and if in his later years he became more overtly regular in his phrasing, this is only a natural result of his increasing time-scale and the immense slowing down of the musical processes involved. It is also the basic reason why the revision of No. 1 was so unsuccessful; Bruckner was no longer able to feel spontaneously the vitality of such ambiguities and irregularities as we have just been examining. As it happens, he left this particular one intact, but there are plenty of others he destroyed, perhaps unknowingly because his mentality, preoccupied with new problems on a vaster scale, was now entirely different.

The drum enters with a crash (letter E) and the music switches violently and impressively from the dominant of E into C, at first neither minor nor major and certainly with no tonic character. It makes as if to be C minor, then brightens to major, only to be grandly supplanted by the E major expected ten bars before. Again Bruckner tends to spoil the effect in the revision by adding the rhythm of Ex. 14, which always benefits, in the Linz version, by the restraint with which it is used. From this climax the music fades away to a silent pause. At this point we might expect A minor, but instead Ex. 15 floats out in the bright key of B major. It hesitates doubtfully. The bass moves mysteriously in upward sequences accompanied by the trill-figure and then, after a themeless pulsing on the dominant of E flat (clarinets, bars

161-2), embarks on an inversion of Ex. 15 in C minor. An extended treatment of this theme ensues, during which the trill-figure creates a rustling forest of sound, mystification increasing as the keys change, gradually darkening into the dominant of A minor. Once more expectations of this key are frustrated, as a vigorous contrapuntal passage breaks out in D minor based on an octave leap, the trill-figure, and an inversion of Ex. 16 (a). The dramatic force of this outbreak is reduced in the revision by the insertion of one bar in the preparation to make the phrasing more regular, and Bruckner knocks out another bar before letter H (for the same misguided purpose) where the music drives magnificently into C minor, which now begins to have the feeling of a tonic. The atmosphere grows wild and stormy. During a brief lull the drum settles on the home dominant, and with real grandeur and tremendous energy the recapitulation sweeps in.

Wisely, Bruckner does not allow an exhaustive recapitulation to destroy the momentum. A brilliant incursion of foreign harmony into the fifth bar of the theme induces a moment of thought before the next passage (on a diminution of the rhythm, as before) begins to rise towards a counterstatement. Before it can reach this, there is a great crunch on combined tonic and dominant harmony (cautiously damped in the revision), and Ex. 15 follows in C major. Not only does Bruckner cushion this crunch in the revision by means of the scoring but again he regularizes the phrasing, softening the shock as well as robbing the entry of Ex. 15 of some of its freshness. The "second subject" itself is shortened, to be swept aside by the *tutti* that originally followed it, and this in turn plunges directly into the *coda* with a sudden *pianissimo* at bar 338, far more exciting than the *diminuendo* of the Vienna score. The *coda* is superb. Beethoven or Schubert would have enjoyed its electric energy and its inevitable sense of climax—indeed its rhythmic power and the exhilarating spin of its self-repeating string figures recall the last movement of Schubert's great C major symphony. Now the rhythm of Ex. 14 comes into its own; in the original version it is much strengthened by not having been previously overdone. A Bruckner finale normally ends with a long-sustained passage on the tonic chord, necessary in the huge time-scale of his later works. The more familiar proportions of this his most "classical" symphony enable him to produce harmonic surprises almost to the very end, which is both punctual and abrupt, made the more thrilling in the Linz version by some irregular periods, including a five-bar penultimate phrase. Every single vital irregularity is removed from the revision, but even worse than this is the putting on of brakes thirty bars from the end, which is thereby crippled into turbid pomposity.* It is the early version that deserves to be played, and frequently; in this form No. 1 is a work of outstanding character. It resembles nothing else, even in Bruckner's music.

* I cannot condemn too harshly those conductors who, when they use the Linz score, add to it the tempo changes of the Vienna version; these were clearly brought in by Bruckner in an attempt to offset the wholesale regularizing of the phrasing in the revision. To use them in the Linz version is to show a crass misconception.

CHAPTER III

SYMPHONY NO. 2, IN C MINOR

As we have seen in discussing the First Symphony, the fears and agitations of Bruckner's latter years resulted in an ill-conceived attempt to modify the early work in the light of his after-development, forgetting that he himself had changed so radically that irrelevancies, incongruities, and unspontaneous untruths would surely accrue. And there is no solution to be found in trying to incorporate in the earlier version what we may think to be improvements in the later; as an exercise it might be interesting, but it can be only an unsatisfactory compromise. With No. 1, however, we have a clear choice between two different widely separated versions, both (so far as we can possibly tell) Bruckner's own—so we must perform either one or the other. The Second Symphony presents another poser, and the solution of this one is less easy to decide. That it can be and has been decided almost as satisfactorily as is humanly possible (by Robert Haas) I have no doubt, but there is room for argument, if only because no available solution can result in perfection. I do not believe that Bruckner himself was ever satisfied that either this or the Third Symphony had reached a definitive form. For that matter the finale of No. 4 is in a similar way. The deep cause is that all three works are transitional. The most tangled situation is in No. 3, because that is the most completely transitional of them all. The Second solves problems of Bruckner's earliest maturity, but with an eye to the future—hence some uncertainties. The Third is itself the beginning of the future—therefore the widespread nature of its inequalities. The fourth very nearly embodies the finest Bruckner, and only its finale has not quite arrived.

The Second Symphony was begun in London in 1871. Bruckner went there to play the organ, and his success prompted him to the remark that "In England my music is really understood". Not that any of his compositions had ever been heard there, but his powers of extemporization must have been impressive. It is ironic to think of the blank reception that England gave his symphonies for so many years, until the 1950s, in fact. He finished the first draft of No. 2 in September 1872, making changes in 1873 and 1877. His final revision, like that of No. 1, belongs to the 1890s. It is not nearly so drastic as the revision of No. 1, though it does contain a suggestion for an appalling new cut in the finale, as well as adding expression markings and fluctuations of tempo. None of these things is advantageous, and we cannot be sure how many of them represent his own real wishes, or simply the promptings of others. If this edition can be rejected, where then is the problem? Should we not stick to the version of 1877? It would be simple if in all honesty we could, but the fact is that the 1877 score was prepared with the help of Johann Herbeck who, devoted and selfless friend though he was, may have prevailed upon Bruckner to make certain cuts. Herbeck died in October 1877; Bruckner was deeply affected by his death, and Robert Haas suggests that it was out of respect for his friend that he allowed the revision to stand. He did, however, carefully keep the earlier version. Haas in his edition (International Bruckner Society, 1938) has restored the excised passages, with indications to that effect. So the problem is not how to make a choice between two different editions, but whether or no to make the cuts, or perhaps one or two of them; a tricky matter. If we admit (as we must) that the work is not perfect either way, why not shorten it? Because to shorten it is to make a hash of the proportions; to do this is not to decrease but to increase the *longueurs*. To perceive the spaces Bruckner wanted to fill satisfactorily is better than to have a work that is too long for the space we would like it to fill. Haas was right. The dropped passages (except perhaps one) should be restored, as I hope now to demonstrate as we explore the symphony.

After all this harping on inequalities in No. 2, it is necessary to describe it as a most beautiful symphony, too little known. The uncertainties are almost confined, as we shall see, to the codas of the first and last movements, and to one passage in the slow movement, and they are not in themselves sufficient reason for neglecting a work that is in most other respects clear and spacious. The fierce unpredictability of No. 1 aroused severe comment that, as always, shook Bruckner's confidence. In the D minor (No. "0") he attempted a smoother, calmer effect and was far from pleased. But calm, patient spaciousness was of all qualities the one he was by nature most fitted to express. He knew it, and the Second is the fruit as well as the expression of his patience, gained in the composition of the three fine masses of the 1860s. The opening has the quiet breadth that we have now come to regard as typically Brucknerian. At the same time there is, as the theme flexes itself, the muscularity that marks the early period. The theme itself is of notable plasticity; its irregularity and unpredictability are of a kind hard to find outside the works of Berlioz. After two bars of soft introductory pulsing on a C minor third in the upper strings, the cellos, in high register, begin a main theme of such singing quality as Bruckner was not to find again until the Seventh. Notice the admirable expansion of the phrase-rhythms—2, 2, 2, 3, 4, 4, 6—twenty-three bars in all, really indivisible, and gathering momentum:

Ex 1 (bar 3)

Although (b) is a variant of (a) it is treated in the *coda* as an idea in its own right, and the other two ideas (c) and (d) have entirely rhythmic consequences. The mixed rhythm of (d) is common in Bruckner. At the end of the theme (letter A)* there is an overlap of periods that subtly confirms the energy at the very moment when the counter-statement begins with the quieter, more regular opening phrases. This invokes a warning that I do not propose to repeat too much in this book, necessary though it often is—do not underestimate this composer!

* Letters and bar-numbers refer to the Haas score.

Ex 2 (bar 24)

Although the key is C minor, the mood could hardly be more different from that of the First Symphony. Here there is serene enjoyment of unassertive music-making, and Bruckner has succeeded in both relaxing and simplifying his invention. In later life he said that at this time he had scarcely the courage to write down "a proper theme" —referring to the way criticism of No. 1 had undermined his confidence and to Otto Dessoff's dismaying question about No. "o"*— but if the Second has no "proper theme", then nothing has. Basses join cellos in the deeper counterstatement and the violins add a flowing line to the richer scoring as the music seems to be turning away from the key into an orthodox transition. The rhythms of Ex. 1 (c) and (d) dominate a *crescendo*; instead of climbing over into a new key, however, we find that on the other side of the hill we are in the home dominant. A long *diminuendo* leaves only a few soft drum taps on G as the rhythm evaporates. At once Bruckner begins his second group in E flat major! It opens with a theme as broad and sweet as the rolling countryside of Upper Austria:

Ex 3 (bar 63)

* See page 20.

The rocking accompaniment turns out to be more important than the cello tune (this symphony, like the Seventh, glorifies the cellos), and the curious "transition" from the dominant of C through silence to plain E flat is eventually the cause of a naïve subtlety in the recapitulation that I never tire of relishing. It will be described in its place, and for the moment we must accept discountenance. Strangely enough the momentum seems to keep going as the theme passes through various harmonies and makes a shapely sentence. It closes into a new, purposeful idea, still in E flat, over a characteristic *ostinato*:

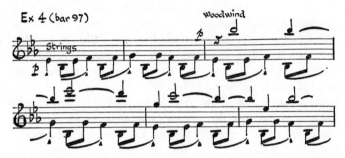

This is the second of five or six themes that form the second group, a long and rich paragraph that describes a contented country full of lively people. The rhythm of the *ostinato* keeps up a glorious swinging stride and as the lungs fill with oxygen, the trumpet-rhythm (Ex. 1 (d)) joins the throng of cheerful sounds. As so often with Bruckner in such passages, themes and figures are constantly transforming themselves into new shapes. After letter D the *ostinato* disperses itself into free counterpoints against a new sustained idea in the woodwind, and by letter E the bass has risen to the surface to become the subject of imitative treatment in G major. But we are not yet in any kind of development, and at letter F still another new theme drifts in, floating on the accumulated momentum of all that has gone before:

G major proves not to be a real key as we swing gently back to E flat, which might never have been disturbed. So the exposition ends, and a masterly piece of work it is, both in the unerring rightness of its proportions and in the freshness of its music. Its close in E flat ponders, and looks in the direction of F minor. Now the development can begin. Ex. 1 (a) returns, at first in F minor, then moving in a distinctly Schubertian manner towards A flat major, where it forms itself easily into comfortable two-bar phrases against a *pizzicato* accompaniment. A *crescendo* evokes a *tutti*, around F minor, with Ex. 1 (a) sounding grandly in imitation at the half-bar. Bruckner then tilts the tonality over into G flat, and there is an unhurried yet exciting hush (bar 233). It is as if we had climbed a hill; the view is suddenly splendid yet calm, and across wide, sunlit spaces an oboe, then a horn, sound a magical augmentation of the *ostinato*. How absurd to try to describe such a moment in a sentence ending with "*ostinato*"! The crass philistinism of the musical analyst was never more cruelly exposed. But we have no choice; the beauty of the music must speak for itself, and we must attempt as well as we can to indicate that Bruckner's mind is working behind his vision. So we must observe that the key is a soft and glowing G flat major and that the *ostinato* soon recovers its normal active measure, joined by a cheerful bassoon counterpoint. The moment of rapt pleasure in the vista must pass, and exhilaration replaces it as we seem to race down the other side of the tonal hill. The music goes through A flat minor into C flat major, which turns to the minor (B minor), to D major (becoming dominant of G), and *fortissimo* to a massive Neapolitan chord of F, on the edge of A minor, with the renewed rhythm of Ex. 1 (d). With a sudden *pianissimo* (letter K) we are in A minor. The *ostinato* is in the bass and Ex. 1 is trying to form in the woodwind. There is a *crescendo*, but it subsides and the basses are left with a *pianissimo*, in the rhythm of the *ostinato*, on the note B. This becomes a major third as Ex. 3 tries to enter in G major; it stops after four bars, again leaving the basses with their B, which now rises a semitone. The C behaves like a major third, and Ex. 3 starts again in A flat. Its rocking accompaniment climbs lazily, and the tune has another easy-going try, now in D flat. Three attempts—G major, A flat, and D flat—and the first one in G makes sure that the A flat and D flat are Neapolitan inflexions of dominant and tonic. So the music drifts quietly on to the home dominant, and the incursion of Ex. 3 guarantees the freshness of Ex. 1, which initiates the recapitulation after a silent pause.

The counterstatement of the main theme takes a new course as it grows into the expected *tutti*. But the *tutti* is shortened abruptly, and is surprisingly twisted back to the home dominant. Why surprisingly? After all, this is what one would expect in a recapitulation. But we remember that in the exposition the first *tutti* also swung back to the home dominant, the second group beginning straight away in E flat, with only a silence as "transition". In view of that curious procedure, we might expect something very different in the restatement, perhaps a smoother but more wide-ranging transition, or a yet more abrupt stroke, such as pausing on the dominant of A minor, then going at once to C major. The latter idea would need some arresting new preparation if it were not to sound, when it arrived, too much like the original; but such strange harmonic procedures would be alien to the nature of this movement. Also alien would be a smooth but involved transition. No, we must have something similar to what happened before, but there must still be that element of surprise that keeps the ears sharpened, and here is the delightfully naïve subtlety mentioned on p. 49. The first surprise is the truncation of the *tutti*, halted on the home dominant. Now consider exactly what Ex. 3 sounded like the first time. We were surprised to hear it in E flat, but not properly surprised until the second note, B flat (see bar 63), because the first chord is G and E flat, both notes still belonging to C minor. The second note tells us that we are in E flat. Having digested this, turn to the restatement. There is the silence after a home dominant chord. Now the surprise is on the *first*, not the second, note of the theme, an E natural! Bruckner's naïve stroke is "obvious", but wonderfully shrewd, and the above laboured attempt to describe it gives no idea of the pleasure it creates. The charming surprise, moreover, is cunningly enhanced by the irregular five-bar period that precedes it, with a three-bar one before that. It is such moments as these that got Bruckner a bad name; but it all depends on how we listen to them—the more attention they get, the more rewarding are they.

So the second group gets under way in the tonic major. As it proceeds Bruckner takes a hint from Beethoven's Ninth Symphony; he allows the second group to slip into the minor, in this case with Ex. 4. Here the *ostinato* is wreathed in new woodwind figures, and the minor tinge gives the whole ensuing paragraph another character. Ex. 5 appears in due course, in E major. Again, its freshness is very simply preserved. E is to C what G was (in the exposition) to E flat, but E major is *not* to C *minor* what G major was to E flat *major*. Time after time we can find these naïve but beautiful strokes in Bruckner. Ex. 4 is a little extended, and the bright E major modestly over-corrects itself until the music hesitates on the dominant of F minor (bars 485–7). Now for the *coda*.

It commences with a quiet but turbulent version of Ex. 1 (b), forming a type of *ostinato* derived from the corresponding place in Beethoven's Ninth. Ex. 1 (a) is placed rhythmically across it and (d) cuts into the orchestra on trumpets. Although the preparation before letter R was on the dominant of F minor, the first entry of Ex. 1 (a) restores C minor, but not quite strongly enough to stand the strain of a final climax. So the *crescendo* fades and the activity is dissipated into a passage that sinks down again, but this time to the dominant of C. This incident was erased from the revised score prepared by Bruckner and Herbeck in 1877—but to begin the *coda* with what was originally a re-start (at letter S) robs the end of its proper tonal foundation. The whole point of the re-starting of the process at this point is that the home dominant is now solidly placed at the base of the structure; so firm is the tonic at this stage that Bruckner is now free to make an impressive excursion through foreign harmony, rising to a dramatic cut-off, a plaintive reminiscence of Ex. 1, then a last C minor *tutti*. The end is rendered very trenchant by a powerful irregularity in bar-grouping—2, 2, 2, 2, 5, 2, 1. For reasons both of proportion and of tonal security, Robert Haas was fully justified in restoring the passage between R and S. His insight into Bruckner is always acute, and even where Bruckner himself has sanctioned an excision, Haas's instinctive understanding often seems to have the effect of posthumously steadying the confidence of a nervous composer, recalling him from dangerously cautious decisions. From a strict musicologist's point of view such an action is reprehensible, but there is no other musicologist who has so far shown one-tenth of Haas's grasp of the artistic problem. In this particular instance Haas's restoration of the passage does not entirely solve the difficulty, for Bruckner's invention is not altogether equal to the occasion in the *diminuendo* before S or in the interruption at T. But with the cut material restored the coda is the right length and its tonal basis is sound; in my view these are decisive considerations. In the first version the ending is at least born punctually; in the revision it is a miscarriage.

Bruckner's control of slow climaxes finds its first mastery in the *Adagio* of this symphony. This skill gave rise to a good many of his finest pieces, not all of them official slow movements. The outline is simple, the mood serene, and the main theme is worked into three great paragraphs, each rising higher, separated by another theme used as a link between them. The key is A flat, and it is never seriously disturbed. The calm main theme opens beautifully in five-part harmony:

Ex.6 Feierlich, etwas bewegt

This first statement brings about no climax. Ex. 6 (b) and its inversion float about and the music drifts almost to a standstill. A new theme scarcely ruffles the static atmosphere:

Ex 7 (bar 34)

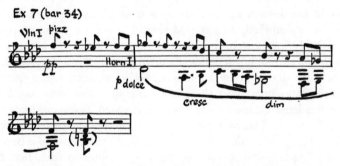

Coming after a C major chord, this seems to begin in F minor, but we cannot feel it as a real key. After only fourteen bars it moves again to the dominant of F (bar 47). In the original score Bruckner now repeats Ex. 7 with a decorative accompaniment and extends the sentence another twenty-two bars before returning to Ex. 6. The revision brings back the main theme at bar 48, but Haas restores the cut passage. For two reasons I would advocate the cut here. First, Bruckner gives us this fine decorated counterstatement later, after the reappearance of Ex. 7, creating a welcome sense of expansion if we have not heard it the first time. Secondly, between letters D and E, in a passage where Bruckner's inspiration is a little torpid, a fearful strain is put on the first horn player; this link, moreover, ends prematurely, giving the unfortunate impression that the horn player has died suddenly of exhaustion, leaving an embarrassed bassoonist to fill up the remaining bars with a feebly improvised *cadenza*. The later treatment of this passage (between letters I and K) successfully avoids this disastrous effect. So with due respect to Haas we will this time adopt the composer's (or possibly Herbeck's) suggestion and go directly from bar 47 to bar 70 (letter E) for the return of the main theme.

The first four bars of Ex. 6 are now elaborated in rich counterpoint that generates a climax before the rest of the theme calmly follows as if nothing had happened. Ex. 7 is resumed, now gently resting on (not in) B flat minor, and its finely scored repeat, with expressive string arpeggios, is much more effective for not having been heard before. With deep feeling, and a hint of the *Benedictus* of the F minor mass, Bruckner comes back once more to the first theme. It is nobly expanded in that immensely broad style this composer made so characteristic, of which this passage is the first notable example. The violins sing a flowing accompaniment; the whole is big and simple, but its inner rhythmic details are complex (and not easy to perform). For the first time in the movement there comes a sense of emotional strain; the serenity is disturbed. At letter M there is a sudden *pianissimo* and a remarkably imaginative four bars of mystery, strikingly anticipating the *Adagio* of No. 9. After this, Ex. 6 (b) is treated, and its consequent. Slowly the activity dies out into a fine drawn *coda*, where spiritual equanimity returns. Now there is a frank quotation from the *Benedictus* (see letter O, and compare with bars 22–26, *Benedictus*, Mass No. 3, in F minor). This *coda* is completely masterly. The perfection with which it gradually reduces the tension until the cloudless end is beyond praise. This is a skill that no one has ever doubted in Bruckner. The tension, however, is not eased for the horn player, nor is the end always cloudless as he tries to control his refractory instrument in the wickedly difficult soft phrases Bruckner's original version asks him to attempt. The revision substitutes a clarinet, for whom the passage is easy. But there is no replacement for the magic of the horn; if we have heard this properly played, we shall be willing to put up with the risk rather than take the easy way out. And if we excuse the horn player that awful ordeal between D and E, perhaps he will reward us in the end.

Before leaving the *Adagio* it is worth while noting a curious difference in periodicity between the 1877 and 1892 editions of the *coda*. The original has the following sequence of bar-groups (from bar 181 onwards)—5, 6, 8, 7, 2, 1. The late revision has 4, 6, 9, 8, 2, 1; the original sequence is one bar less, due to the old man's regularizing of the seven-bar group (third from the end) into eight bars. The first five-bar phrase, beautifully shaped in the original, is truncated to a square four. The duet between flute and solo violin, eight bars in the original, is surprisingly stretched to nine in the revision. It seems to me that in every respect the original is superior; even the eight-bar duet passage sounds irregular and unpredictable because it comes in the wake of 5+6, while its extension by one bar in the revision seems to me merely uncomfortable, following as it does a comparatively stiff 4+6, where eight, though unimaginative, would feel natural. The form of this *Adagio* as a whole, incidentally, is fairly well described by Tovey's generalization; only it and that of the Fifth Symphony may be said to be so.

The Scherzo is a marked advance on those in the previous two symphonies. The theme is terse and malleable:

In the original both halves of the Scherzo (and of the Trio) are repeated, according to classical usage, but not in the late revision. I see no point in removing the repeats, since the movement is not long, and gains from their observance, especially as the return of the Scherzo (when, of course, the repeats are omitted) is lengthened by a *coda* (as in No. 1). Here we find Bruckner's characteristic scherzo broadening out into clear athletic sonata form. There is no separable second group or subject and the dominant minor is solidly fixed only at the double bar. Rhythmically there is more regularity than in No. 1, but this is a sign, not of stiffness, but of the sledgehammer deliberation that Bruckner was eventually to achieve in this part of a symphony. After the double bar he slips into A flat, the first two bars of the theme alternating with a soft rippling four-bar derivative; this at first creates an unusual pattern—2, 4, 2, 4—then the fours return as a new *cantabile* idea forms in the woodwind in E major (letter C) with the rhythm of Ex. 8

in the bass. The music quietens until there is nothing but a unison B, still felt as dominant of E—but the recapitulation bursts in with the sudden violence of a thunderclap. B is only the leading note of C minor, after all!

The relaxed Upper Austrian nature of this symphony is at its most refreshing in the spacious, rather Schubertian Trio, with its lazy yodelling tune:

Ex 9

It makes some delectable modulations as, with a sense of infinite leisure, it casually traces out a form of considerable breadth, and there is something almost majestic in its glorious indolence. But eventually, of course, the return of the Scherzo splits the enchanted ear. The *coda* at the end of it is tremendously succinct and powerful.

Sonata is plainly the basis of the Finale, though its seams are cracked by the pressure from within. This is not to say that the movement is not successful; it is for the most part highly efficient and eminently poetic. But it is the first example of a type in which we see the Brucknerian time-scale making conventional textbook analysis not only difficult, but dangerously misleading. In this case the preservation of a more or less even *allegro* throughout eases matters, and the fact that the second group (Bruckner's *Gesangsperiode*) is not so markedly sectional as it is in some later cases makes it fairly readily assimilable by an overt sonata organism. But the leisurely time-scale is still likely to raise problems for the listener who expects a finale even so classical as those of Bruckner's No. 1 and his posthumous D minor symphony. Although the tempo is a genuine *allegro* the processes are more deliberate even than Schubert's. And we must not be put off by the fact that sometimes the music is so vigorous, producing so strong a sense of movement, that apparent "relapses" into an easy amble are apt to be disconcerting. We have to learn that these naïvely ambling and singing passages are themselves part of a larger motion which, once we have felt its inevitability, can be completely compelling. We learn thereby the reward of patience, and we are composed by Bruckner. To mention these problems here may perhaps exaggerate any present difficulties; this finale is easy to enjoy, and only a certain type of prejudiced professional ear (or, most likely, eye!) might find its procedures questionable. Tovey's "naïve listener" should have no trouble with it, so long as he takes it as it comes and never expects Bruckner to bestir himself too hastily. We begin with a double idea:

The figure marked (a) is obviously connected with Ex. 1 (a) of the first movement (the genesis must be the other way round, as the Finale was composed first). The fragment of scale marked (b) is heard as much in inversion as right way up, and used cunningly and often. A *crescendo* sweeps to an abrupt and formidable theme:

The striding *tutti* suddenly stops with a great thump, as if it had run into some sort of hard object. There is a silent pause. Ex. 10 starts again. Almost as if in fear of the shock with which its enthusiastic career was lately arrested, the music takes a more timid course, without *crescendo*, and blinks hesitantly on (of all places) the threshold of D flat. Another silent pause. Is this some kind of introduction? Clearly we haven't got going yet. Perhaps it's wiser to think of something else while the bruised nose is settling down. So here's a tune, and let's make it the more distracting by having it in an unexpected key. What could be more intriguing than to go straight from the dominant of D flat to A major? And, indeed, what could be better guaranteed to create a sense of movement out of these fits and starts? The tune is, as is proper, naïve and enchantingly beautiful. Already we are forgetting that painfully hard object:

Ex 12 (bar 76)

With a childlike and almost sublime unawareness of problems or obstacles, this heavenly combination circles round and about, settling eventually in E flat (bar 112), its simplicity not quite hiding the fact that it knows this to be a good key to get into. It is, after all, the normal key for the second group of a sonata movement in C minor. More than gratified by this discovery of its delightful and soothing friend, the aggressive Ex. 11, its nose by now having presumably resumed its natural shape and colour, makes a grand entrance in E flat major (letter D). If we treat the music flippantly, we must not lose sight of the fact that this entry of Ex. 11 is really grand; the spacious command of the composer over these elements is not to be argued with. The opening of the movement is powerful and original, and the whole complex generated by Ex. 12 is nothing less than the singing of angels. But Bruckner might well in his simple way have described the music in disconcertingly trivial terms, which would at least have the advantage of being unpretentiously and directly connected with the liveliness of the invention, and perhaps indicate the naïvely potent nature of the forces that bind these disparate elements so surely together.

Ex. 11 is now turned, mostly by sequential-repetitive means, into a large *tutti*, a little stiff in movement (see bars 162–5!) but containing two strongly dramatic moments—when the trumpets are left with the bare rhythm of Ex. 11 (a) (a stroke that looks forward to the *coda* of the

first movement of the Eighth), and when the mass of sound is sharply
cut off at letter F, by which time the harmony has been blasted in the
direction of F minor. A silence—then, starting in G flat, solemn
chorale-like phrases turn out to be another quotation from the F minor
mass (*Kyrie*, bar 122 *et seq.*). These quietly devotional phrases prove to
be a vast cadential passage into E flat major. This is the kind of slowness
on which all else is superimposed, and we begin to understand Bruckner
when we realize that it is the movement of the earth itself that is
constant, not the flurries of activity on its surface. So the first stage of
the design closes in solemn calm, with a broad plagal cadence in E flat.
This is the first of Bruckner's really huge cadential passages; to grasp
the scale of them is important, for they reveal the proportions of all
that has led up to them, as well as committing the composer in advance
to the scale of the rest of the movement. In them is the secret of the
mature Bruckner. If we once comprehend, for instance, that the thirty-
five bars between letters H and I in the finale of the Fifth symphony
are not merely concerned with stating a new theme (the famous
chorale), but function as a gigantic cadence into F major, ending the
first great stage of the movement, we have discovered the vital clue to
the true motion of Bruckner's music. The later symphonies abound
in—no, are founded upon—such cornerstones.

It would be insensitive to resume at once any kind of muscular
activity after so rapt a close and, as always in such cases, Bruckner
continues to ruminate quietly. A flute circles about and a trumpet
softly plays a version of Ex. 1 (d) from the first movement; the outside
world is far away, but not out of reach (it never is with Bruckner,
and we should be careful about attaching too much importance to
romantic writing about his "mysticism"). The key becomes G minor
and something stirs. It is a fascinatingly ingenious new creature, a
cross between Ex. 10 (a) and (b):

Ex 13 (bar 251)

Its first three notes turn themselves into Ex. 10 (a) and the inversion of (b) separates itself (bar 265) and grows a new tail:

It modulates, and in C flat the last two notes of Ex. 14 become the basis of a new melody:

This proves to be a free inversion of Ex. 1 (a), the main figure of the first movement, which duly appears in E flat minor at bar 280. Its second bar is decorated as it continues to modulate:

The decoration (last bar, Ex. 16) gives its rhythm to another new tune, in a curious kind of B major with a flat sixth that soon turns it to the minor:

Out of this new texture, and out of the first two notes of Ex. 10 (b), which rises to the top in its right-way-up version, comes the first bar of Ex. 12. Bruckner is drawing his thematic material together with a vengeance! One can visualize the gleam in Hans Keller's eye. The key changes to F major as Ex. 12 takes over completely. Keys shift about, F minor, A flat, *crescendo*, a pause. Then in G major comes an inversion of Ex. 12 (a). Passing through G flat and a combination with Ex. 1 (a), it slips back on to what is now plainly the dominant of C (letter M). From here a long *crescendo* rises to Ex. 11 in C minor, as pugnacious as ever, and the recapitulation is launched. The same hard object is met with full force, followed by the same stunned pause. Again a new start is made, with Ex. 10. The subtle difference is that Ex. 10 at this instant cannot sound like another start, for it has not led to the last entry of Ex. 11; it therefore sounds like what it really became in the exposition—a transition. As before, it halts on the dominant of D flat. This time, however, Ex. 12 follows with a beautiful harmonic twist into C major, the previous chord treated as German sixth. We not unnaturally expect C major at this point in the restatement, but its effect is even more striking and unexpected than the A major of the exposition, for two good reasons. First, the transition arrived at the dominant of D flat by the same route as before, so we associate it with the previous turn to A major. Second (and this is a point as naïvely clever as that Bruckner made at exactly the same point in the first movement), Ex. 12 started its melody with a C sharp, the third in A major, but the expected note all the same, for C sharp is D flat, and only the soft *pizzicato* A in the bass betrays the deception; in the recapitulation, the first note of the subject (E, the third in C major) is totally unexpected. So does Bruckner make the expected unexpected and adds freshness where it might not be thought possible. In the exposition the whole group moved from one tonal pole (A major) to the other (E flat). Now such discursiveness is unnecessary, and the paragraph is shortened and interrupted by a massive *tutti*.

The powerful outbreak at letter R is completely free from the slight stiffness that at first marred its counterpart in the exposition. It expands in a manner at once formal and unbridled into a magnificent full orchestral sweep, mightily determined upon C minor, yet with impetus enough to thrust its way this side and that. Ex. 11 is forged into a new and flashing weapon:

Ex 18 (bar 513)

But the music seems to lose sight of C minor, and the *tutti* explodes in short bursts of rage, soon calmed by the quotation from the *Kyrie* of the F minor mass, leading back to the home dominant. Regrettably, the return of this quotation was removed from the revision (bars 540–62 in the original), thus spoiling one of the most poetic strokes in the work. There follows some softly excited play with a *pizzicato* treatment of Ex. 10 (b), confirming the tonal direction towards home, and the *coda* begins with an impressive groundswell on Ex. 10 (a), C minor firmly seated.

Above the groundswell Ex. 10 (b) is turned into an *arpeggio*. The power of the music is greatly increased by the fact that it now strides in periods of three bars before broadening to five, then four, and tightening compellingly to a series of twos when it reaches a fierce *fortissimo*. It shows signs of driving into G minor, but the drum hurls out an imperious "No!", and halts everything with a reverberating C. Now there is a gap, during which wistful distant voices are heard reminiscing on Ex. 1 and 12. Then the groundswell begins again. This time it rises swiftly to a climax in C major and the symphony is over. The 1877 revision makes a bad cut in this *coda*; the whole process from the first inception of the groundswell to the end of the reminiscent passage is removed, rendering the C major climax at the end even more maddeningly premature than the revised ending of the first movement. We may justifiably regret that Bruckner did not think of something more convincing than those reminiscences as a means of bridging the gap between the argument about tonality (ended by the drum at bar 638) and the final onset of the C minor groundswell at letter Z. But there must be a gap here; to start the groundswell again immediately without thinking about the matter would be crass, and Bruckner was right to feel it so. He did not solve the problem, and it would be wrong to attempt to solve it for him with either a rude cut or a politely sophisticated transition. We must put up with things as they are. In the 1892 revision (which I have almost ignored in this analysis) there is an insane proposal to cut the whole of the recapitulation. Now that we have considered the structure of the movement and some of its many subtleties, I hope it is not necessary to comment in detail on suggestions of this nature.

CHAPTER IV

SYMPHONY NO. 3, IN D MINOR

Of all Bruckner's symphonies the Third poses the most problems, textual and structural. Its opening, cautiously anticipated in No. "o", opens new prospects; but the work often falters. It is so far the grandest and most individual Bruckner symphony, but it is much less successfully constructed than Nos. 1 or 2. No version is satisfactory, and the last score of 1888–9 (purporting to be the composer's own revision, so far as can be ascertained) is in some respects an even sadder piece of interesting butchery than the final score of No. 1. The history is as follows. The very first version dates from 1873, altered somewhat in 1874, and has never been published. At this time Bruckner was more obsessed with Wagner's music than at any other time in his life, and the symphony contained a number of deliberate quotations from, mainly, *Tristan und Isolde*, *Die Walküre* and *Die Meistersinger*. This was the version Wagner saw and of which he accepted the dedication; Bruckner sent him a fair copy of the 1874 score. A further revision (1876–7), with the direct Wagner quotations removed, was performed in 1877. Herbeck was to have conducted it, but died, and Bruckner had to direct the performance himself. It was the most frightful experience of his life. He was not an expert conductor, nor did he possess the kind of personality that could overcome a lack of technical skill by winning the understanding of the orchestra. The playing was (presumably) inadequate, the audience left in large numbers during the symphony, and many of those that stayed did so to laugh or hiss. At the end only a handful were left, and to complete the poor man's utter humiliation, the orchestra walked off and left him alone on the platform. If Bruckner had enjoyed the confidence of a Napoleon he might have been upset by all this; how it must have affected his nervous, retiring nature is beyond imagining. Fortunately for him, the publisher Theodor Rättig had been at some of the rehearsals and, undeterred by the fiasco of the concert, offered to publish the work.

In 1878 the score was printed, together with a piano duet arrangement by Gustav Mahler (then seventeen) and Rudolf Krzyzanowski. The score contained alterations in which Bruckner, shattered by the failure of the work, acquiesced only too easily. (An unadulterated publication, edited by Fritz Oeser, was issued by the International Bruckner Society in 1950.) The Rättig edition aroused very little interest at the time, and the symphony seems to have been shelved. In 1888–90 Bruckner returned to it again, somewhat reluctantly, pressed by Franz and Joseph Schalk. He had recently experienced another severe disappointment, the rejection of No. 8 by Hermann Levi, the cause perhaps of most of the agitated revising of his last years. When Mahler heard that No. 3 was being revised again he implored Bruckner not to do it. The composer, always impressionable, changed his mind again and told the publisher he wanted the old score to be reprinted. In the meantime, engraving for the new version had already been started, and fifty new plates had therefore to be destroyed, at considerable loss to the long-suffering Rättig. The Schalks now returned to the fray, and the revision went ahead, Bruckner's change of mind being "vetoed personally" by Joseph.* There is no doubt that the ferocious cuts and new transitions in the Finale of the 1890 version are the work of Franz.† Bruckner accepted them, and it has been argued that therefore they are sacrosanct. But in the state of mind he was in at that time (and often at other times, too) Bruckner would have accepted almost anything. I have no wish to attack the Schalk brothers and some of the other friends who advised Bruckner. Most of them were brilliant, experienced, and sincere musicians who wanted only to help. But they were too close to events to see the problems clearly. Mahler may have been wrong in asserting that the 1878 score was not in need of attention; he could, however, see that the vacillating confusion of the composer was increased rather than eased by the chorus of willing assistants, and he was right to propose that matters be left alone. There must have been some animosity between him and the Schalks and this, too, cannot have improved Bruckner's peace of mind. Ultimately the blame can be only Bruckner's, for not resolutely dismissing all these distractions. The responsibility was his alone.

The result is that we are faced with two published versions and must choose between them. To try to achieve a compromise between them is useless because the faults of 1878 are mostly made worse by the emendations of 1889, and where the later score makes really interesting

---

* See Leopold Nowak's preface to the 1890 score, published under his editorship by the Bruckner Society in 1958.

† See Nowak's preface, referred to in the previous footnote.

changes, they are by the composer of the Eighth Symphony. The score of 1878 is stylistically purer, and though its construction leaves much to be desired, its weaknesses are exacerbated, not propped, by the crude remedies of the later version. We shall consider both, though not in minor detail; that would demand a book in itself, and who would read it?

In September 1873, Bruckner took the Second Symphony and the first draft of No. 3 to Wagner, and begged permission to dedicate one of them to him. At first patronizing, Wagner suddenly was impressed by the opening of the Third. The next day poor Bruckner, still bemused by having actually been in the Presence, was unable to remember which symphony the Master had chosen and had to write Him a note, asking Him. Wagner confirmed that it was the one with the trumpet theme, and always referred afterwards to "Bruckner the trumpet". Despite his lofty amusement and the fact that he really did very little in a practical way for Bruckner, he had a genuine respect for the curious Austrian and once remarked that he was the only symphonist who approached Beethoven. If one looks at the opening of the Third Symphony, it is not hard to see why he thought this. There is an influence behind it far stronger than Wagner's—the mysterious beginning of Beethoven's Ninth. The two openings are not really similar, except superficially in atmosphere, but a comparison between them can be revealing in that it shows Bruckner's very different time-scale and the originality with which he is able to accept so mighty an influence. Beethoven's opening embodies a single idea, the rapid formation of a classical *allegro* theme out of fragments drawn with immense and increasing energy from a mysterious hush. It happens very quickly, and we are not long in doubt that this is a classical *allegro* of unprecedented power and mobility. Bruckner's beginning is also in an awed hush. Looming dimly through a deep mist of floating figurations is a broad and simple trumpet theme:

Ex 1 (bar 5)

With marked gradualness a climax is built. But there is no question of fragments forming a main theme—we have already, before even the *crescendo*, heard a complete theme, so what is to happen at the end of the *crescendo*? The answer is a completely different theme, in massive unison, followed by a soft inverted question:

Ex 2 (bar 31)

Notice the silent pause after the first phrase of Ex. 2. Bruckner knows that he could not now, even if he wished (which he does not), establish an *allegro* tempo. This is an altogether different scale. We shall find the same situation, with even more enormous proportions, in the opening of Bruckner's Ninth Symphony. It may seem at first sight a strange paradox that Beethoven takes sixteen bars before we are made aware of a thematic entity, while Bruckner in both the Third and the Ninth produces one after only four bars. But the presence of a complete theme at an early stage can only delay matters, and so Bruckner in No. 3 has to use thirty bars before reaching the climax, and in No. 9, sixty-two.

Ex. 2 is not quite unprepared; its first two notes are anticipated by a repetitive figure in woodwind and horns as the *crescendo* mounts. Its *fortissimo* phrase is now repeated, but impressively harmonized; each time this phrase appears in the movement it is given more remarkable harmony. The soft questioning is then extended sequentially, and a sudden burst thrusts towards the dominant, where the process begins again. Here is another notable difference between Bruckner's and Beethoven's procedures. Beethoven starts with an open fifth (A and E), revealed as the dominant of D minor when the main theme emerges and, after a *tutti*, resumes the opening in the tonic, which then turns dramatically to B flat major when the theme crashes out for a second time. Bruckner begins in the tonic, not an open fifth but plain D minor, and there is no ambiguity; he then reverses Beethoven's tonal order by making the counterstatement start from the dominant. This, too, shows the gulf between Beethoven's muscular athleticism and Bruckner's statuesque juxtaposition of masses. The counterstatement is not exact; Ex. 1 is not permitted to complete itself (there are limits, even in this time-scale!) and the harmony is more mobile as the *crescendo* rises in twenty bars to Ex. 2 (10 bars less than before). With Ex. 2 there is a powerful wrench into dissonant harmony in a sort of B flat minor; but it is insecure, and the quiet companion phrase is even more questioningly uncertain of its direction. But it does seem as if we are to go into B flat. Instead, at bar 101* a German sixth is unexpectedly resolved into F major, and the second group begins with a complex of lyrical ideas, pervaded by the mixed rhythm of twos and threes of which Bruckner is so fond:

Both (a) and (b) are equally important and it is a pity that they are scored in such a way that their outlines easily become confused; they frequently cross when the tone colours of the two lines are insufficiently contrasted, so that they defeat each other. This is a common fault in the scoring of this symphony and is symptomatic of a desire for fussy detail, betraying unsureness in the work. Bruckner was probably aware that he was entering new territory and his nervousness is evident in a thousand details as well as in the structure itself. Partly consequent upon the superfluity of detail and partly upon the type of faulty scoring we have just observed, this *Gesangsperiode* fails to sing as broadly as it ought. (There is, incidentally, an abominably coarse alteration at bar 159 in the 1890 score.) There are exquisite moments in passing as this section modulates freely about, but I have yet to hear a performance in which a real continuity of line is established. Eventually, however, it gathers itself together and the key of F is confirmed by a splendid swinging theme, imperiously masterly in its breadth and power:

* Bar numbers refer to the 1878 version, edited by Fritz Oeser.

The music sweeps into a grand chorale-like passage and a climax on the dominant of A, with a version of Ex. 1 in imitation between trombones and horns. Is this vast exposition going to end, after all, in A major and not F major? So it seems as everything falls away in that direction, though not without suggestions of C major, the dominant of F. Just as the question appears to be settled in favour of A major (bar 241), however, there is a marvellous cadential return to F major, and the exposition ends in sublime calm.

So far it is all (with some reservations about the first paragraph of the second group) great music, the finest and most compelling Bruckner had yet composed. No wonder Rättig was impressed at its rehearsal, and it says much for his generous faith in the composer that he was not put off by what must have been a chaotic event. There is no loss of grandeur as the development begins in quiet mystery with a turn to F minor (bar 261), then a resumption in that key of the fascinating opening. Dark modulations are questioned by Ex. 2 (b), moving towards a pause on the dominant of A (bar 297). In A minor a *pizzicato* inversion of one of the opening string figurations serves as background to a plaintive treatment of Ex. 2 (a) which becomes more and more insistent as a climax is built up. In the 1878 score a lively new figure is brought in (violins, bar 323); it was removed in 1889 and the whole *crescendo* rescored with a gain in clarity but a loss in interest. In both versions the culmination is a huge unison delivery of Ex. 1 by the full orchestra in D minor.

This is where Bruckner's serious troubles begin. Neither in 1878 nor in 1890 were they solved though, as we shall see, he found the way out in the first movement of the Ninth (completed, significantly, after the attempt to revise No. 3). The old accusation, that Bruckner made the fatal mistake of sticking haplessly to sonata form when the matter in hand was unsuitable for it, is here not without justice, though I would prefer to apply the stricture in a slightly different way. Although the time-scale of this movement is very broad and shows few signs of the kind of action characteristic of sonata, it can still, up to the point we have reached, be construed as an immensely slow but coherent sonata scheme. If one gets used to the slowness and the way the music is delivered in large *quanta*, so to speak, the great length of the second group can be accepted as a proportionate expansion of the vast opening. Even the fact that much of this second group is built of small four-bar bricks is not really a serious obstacle, since it is possible to feel them accumulating momentum once we have got rid of classical preconceptions. Any doubts as to the scale of Bruckner's intentions are finally dispelled by the entry and subsequent direction of Ex. 4, which once more fills the great sails and gets the ship under way after a nearly becalmed period. What follows is obviously a development, yet surprisingly terse under the circumstances. Up to the entry of Ex. 1 at bar 341, in the tonic, we have the following proportions—exposition, 256 bars, development, 83 bars. At the top of an imposing *crescendo* we find Ex. 1 being declaimed in the unmistakable home tonic with the majesty of the full orchestra. What more natural than our assumption that here is the recapitulation?

Anyone who knows how difficult it is to compose (as contrasted with the ease of writing plausible newspaper criticism) will understand that the development has not hitherto created sufficient momentum of its own to carry such a statement as this. Bruckner himself knows this, but is unable to see a convincing way out of the difficulty. The trouble is that Ex. 1 is itself static and square, and brings matters to a halt. To carry such an idea with the sense of forward movement vitally necessary would require a far bigger head of steam than the development has so far generated. Things are made worse, moreover, when the sense of dead weight is made finally unmanageable by the continuation in stolidly square phrases with no more movement in them than in the average national anthem. The fatal mistake is that Bruckner has it fixed in his head that he wants his real recapitulation to begin with the mysterious opening of the movement. The intended function of the *fortissimo* version of Ex. 1 in the tonic is threefold: (*a*) to bring back a sense of the tonic at a point before things have got too far for it ever to be restored satisfactorily, (*b*) so to provide a solid tonal background for the official recapitulation, which he has decided will begin 80-odd bars later, and (*c*) to mark the central climax of the development and hence of the movement as a whole. Unfortunately the intentions and the reality do not coincide because the problems of momentum in a sonata movement on this scale and with this kind of slowness have defeated the composer at this stage in his development.

As if Bruckner realizes that there is now but a faint hope of saving the situation, he plunges on with the *tutti* beginning at bar 341, rather desperately whipping up the rhythm of Ex. 1 in half then quarter diminution, with forced modulations. The 1890 revision interposes a *piano* at bar 373 and rewrites the rest of the *tutti* in the style of No. 8; this is momentarily impressive, but no more successful in dealing with the root problem. In both cases the music finds itself stamping up and down in the mud, is unable to proceed, and stops. The 1878 version then brings in a worried reference to Ex. 2 (b) followed by a bit more frustrated stamping in A flat minor (2 bars); further sequences on Ex. 2 (b) lead to F major and a glance at Ex. 3 and a scarcely explicable resurrection of the theme of the first movement of the Second Symphony (no doubt it would be possible to discover some ingenious thematic connection here, but it could bring no blinding revelation of larger purpose, sufficient to make everything else convincing. It would rather seem to me that Bruckner's nerves had finally got the better of him). From here there is a solemn descent to the home dominant and the official recapitulation. The 1890 score has a cut in the foregoing passage, going straight from the first halt in the big *tutti* to the reminiscence of Ex. 3; this is worse—the original at least lets us down in stages, but this amounts to an incontinent collapse.

The recapitulation provides few surprises. How can it when it has been robbed of the energy that alone can generate them? There is, however, one magnificent stroke, yet another harmonization of Ex. 2 (a) (bar 459–61) so powerfully original as to make one catch the breath. There is no counterstatement of the first group, and the second begins in D major at bar 481, culminating as before in Ex. 4 (bar 547). Towards the end of the paragraph the two editions diverge again in preparing for the *coda*. That of 1878 constructs a well-proportioned *tutti* that arrives at the home dominant by way of fine modulations (see bar 557 *et seq.*). The 1890 alteration starts at bar 559 (the revised movement is in fact a couple of bars longer than the original) and the *tutti* now amounts to two short four-bar bursts in F major and A major which sound comparatively unmotivated. In the *coda* itself only details are changed and it begins impressively with touching homage to Beethoven's Ninth in the form of a chromatic *basso ostinato*. The *crescendo* rises soon to *ff* and the bass strides formidably downwards to a B flat, then A, then G sharp, on which last a diminished seventh is raised, and cut off. Ex. 2 (b) intervenes with a final question, then the last D minor *tutti* breaks out. Bruckner increases the tempo in an attempt to give it greater impact, but the fact is that without the momentum that was lost half-way through the movement nothing has had real spur, and the end has a hollow ring. He has entered a new world, but has not yet found his way about it.

The slow movement contains two fine themes and the beginning of another. The abortive one, unfortunately, is the first which, after

Ex.5

the noble first four bars rather loses its way, drifting into a series of haplessly romantic one-bar sequential repetitions, made the more tedious by the somewhat cloying insistence on an *appoggiatura*, formed from (d) (which is itself not an *appoggiatura*) and combined with a derivative of (c). The key is E flat major, a striking effect after the previous D minor movement, which has not exploited large-scale Neapolitan relationships to any great extent. But its beauty is marred, I think, by its obscuration so soon by the feverish and highly coloured harmonic changes that follow from the ninth bar, almost mawkish in character. With deadly insistence the one-bar phrase wails and batters its way to a *fortissimo* of pedestrian fervour, once interrupted by a calm thought that reminds us we are still listening to Bruckner:

Ex 6 (bar 20)

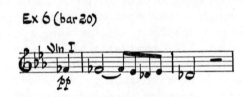

This takes over, and flows into an inorganic cadential link that confirms the original E flat. Then with a change to triple time and a more active tempo comes a new theme of real Brucknerian quality, a blessed relief:

Ex 7 (bar 41)

B flat major is its key, and its wide tonal range does nothing to undermine the fact. It is counterstated with beautiful syncopated decorations in the violins, but hesitates before the expected close. In G flat, slower (*misterioso*), there follows a simple theme, chaste in feeling:

Ex 8 (bar 73)

It is treated at some length, not quite coherently, first falling into extensions of its semiquaver figure that are just a little automatic. The keys change with more than a suspicion of the haphazard, and a *forte* contrapuntal development of the two crotchets of its second bar is narrowly rescued from academic stagnation by the return of Ex. 7, starting in C major with the air of "As I was saying before we got into this muddle". The blood begins to circulate again and a rich paragraph grows to a quiet climax with Ex. 7 given almost a full statement in E flat—in the 1878 score. In the revision Bruckner must have felt that this E flat major unduly forestalled the return of the main theme, and he made the passage stop short of it, merging rather clumsily into a *gauche* transition. I do not feel that the return to the tonic and the first theme are spoiled by hearing Ex. 7 in E flat; it does not at that point sound like a tonic, yet it serves to place it in the ear. The actual transition of 1878 is not very well organized, but though too long, it is harmonically more interesting than that of 1890. So, after the meandering and intermittently inspired and beautiful middle section, we return (perhaps with some trepidation) to the opening.

This is where Bruckner, in an *Adagio*, may normally be expected to raise a climax. One shudders to think of those wailings and batterings and of the hideous heights to which they might be goaded if a similar but bigger bug now bites the composer. Luckily he builds on the main theme a *crescendo* of genuine majesty, ending in great blocks of sound separated by Ex. 6. In 1890 he added to these blocks a trumpet line that Oeser is quite right in describing as not among his noblest inspirations. Was it Franz Schalk's, I wonder? The *coda* is solemn and peaceful, of fine draughtsmanship, including an oblique reference to the "sleep" motive from *Die Walküre*.

The Scherzo is the first that Bruckner begins *pianissimo*. In most other respects it belongs, however, to his earlier rather than his late manner, and there are three main thematic germs in its opening section:

The figure (c) grows from both (a) and (b). The first part ends on the dominant (the movement is in D minor) and after the double bar turns into B flat major with Ex. 9 (a) used as accompaniment to a graceful new *Ländler*:

A cloud comes over it and we return to D minor for a restatement that ends in the tonic. The Trio is another *Ländler*, in A major; there is a distinct whiff of Austrian beer:

The slight tipsiness of this music becomes downright alcoholism at the end of the first section, where it reels, rooted to the spot, with hiccuping one-bar repetitions. The same condition obtains at the end.

If this Trio is played with gusto it has much gaiety, though it suffers
severely from congestion. The texture is frequently muddled and over-
loaded, and the effect is bound to be sometimes messy however much
care is taken to clarify it in performance. To play it slower than the
Scherzo makes it insufferably windy, yet at the pace it demands the
detail must inevitably get blurred. This is simply a roundabout way of
saying it is not well written.

With the Finale we return once more to insoluble structural problems. Against racing string quavers in the formation—

the brass attack the tonic from an acute angle with a blazing theme in
the same rhythm as Ex. 1:

This is an exciting start, and it comes in two waves, the second ending
in the tonic major and dying away. As it does, we begin to wonder if
it really is the tonic, not a dominant. But it would be odd indeed to
go full pelt into the subdominant so early in the movement. Bruckner
evades the issue, and it is sheer delight when the second theme appears
in an unexpectedly radiant F sharp major. Here we discover the famous
double theme which is the subject of a conversation recorded by August
Göllerich, Bruckner's pupil and first biographer. He and the composer
were walking one evening past the Schottenring when they heard the
gay music of a ball from inside a house. Nearby was the Sühnhaus,
where lay the body of the cathedral architect Schmidt. Bruckner said,
"Listen! There in that house is dancing, and over there lies the master
in his coffin—that's life. It's what I wanted to show in my Third
Symphony. The polka means the fun and joy of the world and the

chorale means its sadness and pain." The polka and the chorale are combined, the latter forming a rich and solemn background on the soft brass to the former on the strings:

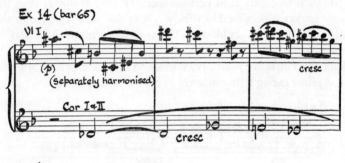

Even in this felicitous inspiration there are traces of that unclear writing which seems to dog this symphony. The crossing of the two violin parts and the A sharp of the violas create a difficult situation, not solved even by judicious adjustment of the dynamics:

Despite Bruckner's remarks, the predominant effect of this passage is of an easy-going cheerfulness, and it proceeds with charming casualness in four-bar phrases as he knowingly avoids full closes and inserts a six-bar period here and there; a square self-completing tune would have been fatal. Eventually he finds himself comfortably in an orthodox F major (bar 125), and towards the end of the section the flowing harmonic accompaniment in the wind (which has long given up trying to be a chorale) is beginning to assume the rhythm of the second bar of Ex. 13. Suddenly there is the powerful and severe interruption of a third theme:

Ex 16 (bar 155)

Against this impressively disjointed unison the 1878 score has what Erwin Doernberg well describes as a "firm counter-unison" in the brass, in a rhythm that eventually gives rise to frank derivatives of Ex. 13. In 1889 only the fag-end of this was left in the subsequent *diminuendo*, depriving it of point. The quick *diminuendo* on the dominant of B flat minor turns aside to a C major that is really the dominant of F, where Ex. 16 develops soft transformations of itself. But it soon blazes up again into a *tutti*, which is sensibly relieved, in the 1890 score, of a not very successful interruption in the form of a momentary hush. The *tutti* breaks off on a chord of G flat which proves to be the flat supertonic in F major, where soft cadences on the horns make a settled close.

As in the first movement Bruckner has produced a huge stretch of music that can just be construed as a sonata exposition. This one, however, is even stranger, because it is, as it were, thrown out in chunks, great slabs of contrasting musical masonry placed in blunt juxtaposition with airy gaps between them. There is something fascinating about this method which, in the mature Bruckner, is by no means crude or amateurish. Its essence is deeply opposed to the sonata principle of continuous muscular tonal action; it is like Stonehenge compared with the settlements in which its makers lived. In this early example of Bruckner's *genre*, the achievement is not always pure; there are a few mud huts among the colossal stones.

Soon the matter of Ex. 13 returns in a weighty and stormy development, eventually subsiding on the dominant of C after Ex. 1 from the first movement has been hurled in with all possible force (bar 341). As in the previous large *tutti* near the end of the exposition, the action is clarified and given greater continuity in the 1890 version; many details are re-written and the whole passage is invested with greater harmonic strength. But both versions are left with the same problem —how to make a recapitulatory climax? In the first movement the entry of Ex. 1 in D minor without sufficient momentum behind it created an impossible situation. Its appearance at this juncture in the Finale was a temptation Bruckner would have done well to resist. There is certainly far more momentum now than there was in the first move- ment, perhaps enough to carry even this obstinately square theme, but the abrupt introduction of its plain diatonicism into a development getting its driving force from chromatic inflexions, added to the fact that it nails down the dominant of a foreign key, is more than the momentum can support. There is a horrible finality about this theme, almost as embarrassing when it is insisting on a dominant as when it is affirming a tonic. So everything grinds to a halt, like a steamroller encountering a road-block. The driver can only get out and have a look round and, if the steamroller is not too badly damaged, try to go some other way. The regrettable thing is that Bruckner, the driver, put the infernal road-block there himself. He could have had a clear road and driven his vehicle with a fine head of steam uninterrupted to D minor.

Instead he has to get out and inspect the damage; the machine is bent, alas, and can henceforth go but by fits and starts. So it is for the rest of the piece. Once the vast slow momentum of a Bruckner movement is broken, there is little hope of recovering it. Revising cannot help, at least not the kind of revising Bruckner carried out in this case. The only thing for him to have done would have been to go back to the point where the impetus was lost, or perhaps a little before it, and compose afresh to the end. And no one else could have helped him—certainly not the friends who proffered advice while he fiddled feverishly with the works. And cuts are no good—if a machine crocks up, you will never get it to go by hacking lumps off it.

Let us, however, abandon these diverting analogies and get back to the music. We have collapsed on the dominant of C and must do what we can. In C minor a mournful version of the chorale with *pizzicato* accompaniment potters gloomily about until, in the 1878 version, Bruckner violently kicks it out of the way with the very passage that should have come as the climax of the previous ill-fated *tutti*—the recapitulation of Ex. 13 in D minor. Why then cannot we make a cut, and graft this on to the previous *tutti* in place of Ex. 1? Because it would

mean redirecting the harmonic trend for some considerable time before
letter S (where Ex. I entered) in order to ensure the security of the
tonic, and only Bruckner could have done that. It would be possible
to find a place where a join could be made without too much internal
surgery, but it would not be composition, and I sincerely hope that
no conductor who might have been given this book as a present by his
worst enemy will get the idea of attempting it.

The 1890 revision makes far worse nonsense than that. From the
abortive doodling with the chorale it goes direct to the recapitulation
of Ex. 14, and the crass tautology that results has to be heard to be
believed. In the 1878 version the two things are at least decently separated by the big *tutti* at bar 379, and cannot form the kind of incestuous
union that was later perpetrated, presumably by Franz Schalk. And
in the earlier score the proportions are roughly right, even if the
construction is ramshackle.

After the recapitulation of Ex. 14, which begins in A flat major
(bar 433), the rest of the movement really does go by fits and starts,
as if the composer knows that there is no hope of recapturing momentum. But his sense of proportion is still active, and he knows exactly
what time he is due to arrive at the end. In the 1878 version we have a
phenomenon rather like that of a bus driver who, though he is early,
is determined to arrive at the terminus on time and who therefore
hangs about at each stop. I am well aware that this somewhat dismal
analogy does not fit with the previous one of a steamroller that must
arrive late because it has injured itself in an argument with a road-
block. If we want to return to that one, we might observe that the
steamroller could have gone much farther more easily if it had
remained in good working order. Strangely enough, there is something
rather impressive and powerful in the massive ejaculatory last few
minutes of this symphony in its earlier version,* much more acceptable
than the crude truncation of the later piece of butchery, in which the
triumphant blaze of D major on Ex. I comes with all the bombast
and prematurity of a victory forecast by a notoriously horizontal
heavyweight. In both versions the end is preceded by an empty fanfare,
not mitigated by the fact that an augmentation of Ex. 13 is present
to give it a semblance of respectability, and containing a dreadful
penultimate dominant thirteenth, but the ending of 1878 is at least
punctual, even if the journey has been rough. The Third is the weakest

* Though it would be hard to find a good excuse for the arbitrary quotation
of Ex. 3 at bar 555.

of Bruckner's numbered symphonies; if I have seemed to treat it at times unkindly, I hope also to have made it apparent that its flaws are of the kind inherent in a characteristic work of discovery as well as that it contains many beauties. Without it the later masterpieces could not have existed.

CHAPTER V

SYMPHONY NO. 4, IN E FLAT MAJOR
(Romantic)

To TURN TO the clean lines and structural mastery of the first three
movements of the Fourth Symphony is a great relief after the com-
plications and uncertainties of No. 3. In the Third Bruckner was
struggling to understand certain instincts of his own that ran counter
to his experience and knowledge of the sonata-symphony. Only a
faint glimmer of the truth emerged, and the work suffers from a kind
of artistic schizophrenia. The difficulty occurs again in the Finale of
No. 4, but the solution is nearer. He was trying to find a new type of
Finale of such extraordinary nature that he fully achieved it only twice,
in the Fifth and Eighth Symphonies, each very different from the other,
but both sharing an essence hard to describe. We shall attempt to
describe it in due course; meanwhile we must observe how Bruckner,
for the time being turning his back on these intractable matters, made
a new attack on pure sonata composition in the first movement of the
Fourth, attaining a skill and sureness, a simplicity and depth of expression, unprecedented in his work. It is as if he felt he could not win
mastery in one field without first confirming it in the other.

Like its companions, the Fourth went through various vicissitudes.
Its earliest version was written between January and November 1874
(while Bruckner was also making the first revisions of No. 3). During
the next three years the Fifth was being composed and the Third
revised for the second time. These tasks completed, Bruckner returned
to No. 4, making a new score between January and September 1878.
But in December of the same year he wrote an entirely new scherzo
(the one we are familiar with now); then between November 1879
and the following June he totally recast the Finale. This is the version
(1878–80) published in 1936 by the International Bruckner Society
under the editorship of Robert Haas, and later reprinted with small
amendments and corrections by Leopold Nowak. The first published
edition, however, was issued by Gutmann in 1889. It contains
an immense number of alterations in scoring and considerable cuts in
the Scherzo and Finale, carried out, so far as can be divined, in 1887–8.
Bruckner must have acquiesced in this, but nearly all the changes bear

the stamp of Franz Schalk and Ferdinand Loewe, who saw the work through the press. The orchestration is made more Wagnerian, the clean-cut character of the original is fogged by mixed colours and tempo changes, and the cuts make nonsense (Tovey approved of the one in the *reprise* of the Scherzo but it seems to me crude and insensitive). One can find many similarities between these changes and those made in the first publication of the Fifth Symphony, which Bruckner is known not to have supervised. The only version of No. 4 that is more or less above suspicion is that of 1878–80, which is the one I propose to deal with here.

The Fourth is the only one of Bruckner's symphonies with a title, and we need not take that too seriously, for it has little more significance than the amusingly naïve "programmes" to the symphonies with which the composer was wont to entertain his friends. His explanations were always *ex post facto*, and the music itself renders them trivial. Exactly what Bruckner meant by "romantic" may perhaps be guessed from the picturesque terms in which he afterwards described No. 4 (medieval town, dawn, knights, hunting scene, etc.); the music is so much more than this! On the other hand, nineteenth-century romanticism, with its accent on emotional egotism inflated into a tormented would-be humanism, has nothing to do with Bruckner, who could not understand or share the postures of his time. It was this kind of romanticism that lay behind the falsifications of his scores, and in so far as the title of the symphony may have encouraged the more exaggeratedly subjective type of conductor (such as Furt-wängler, for instance), it can have been nothing but a disadvantage to the work. If we define romanticism as a flight from reality (an over-simplified but not meaningless way), we can find nothing in this symphony so romantic as some passages in the Ninth, where the desperate and ailing composer seems to be trying to reach beyond the grave. No. 4 is an eminently salubrious work. Bruckner is really romantic only when his artistic vision is insufficiently focused to allow him to be realistic about his aims; it is then that we find him tending to employ harmony and scoring typical of a lower and more egocentric plane, as for example in the opening paragraph of the *Adagio* of the Third Symphony, with its drearily moping *appoggiature* and blatant modulations, or in a few passages in his late music. We had better forget the title of No. 4; it leads us away from the music.

The beginning is magically beautiful, and I do not propose to try to rival the many attempts there have been to describe it in poetic terms.

It is one of the deepest and most instantly compelling symphonic openings since Beethoven:

Ex 1

Notice the superb bass line from bar 12 onwards, and the airy effect when cellos and basses cease in bar 19, where the woodwind take over the theme. The horn follows them with echoing imitations; passing through rich shades of tonality, the music slowly opens out. Bruckner's favourite mixed rhythm of two and three adds life to it and becomes the basis of a splendid *tutti*, affirming the key of E flat:

Ex 2 (bar 51)

This opening is even broader than that of No. 3; it takes fifty bars to reach the first *tutti*, as compared with thirty in the other. Yet it is far more economical thematically and moves with greater certainty. Harmonically it is more active and the remarkable breadth of the horn theme establishes a majestically deliberate sense of movement from the very start. There is no trace of stiffness in the use of four-bar phrases, which develops a huge quiet swing, and the fact that the *tutti* maintains the same great stroke means that in spite of the activity we can still feel the calm rhythm of Ex. 1, like the regular motion of a ship with variously animated life on deck. Stiff periods can be a nuisance in Bruckner (as we shall find in parts of the Finale of this work), but here they are a deep unifying factor, the easy swell of the sea on which the ship sails.

The *tutti* lasts for twenty-two bars, first turning into the minor and moving to C flat major. A characteristic progression culminates on the dominant of B flat, the normal and expected key for the second group. English readers will be familiar with Tovey's essay on this symphony in Volume II of his *Essays in Musical Analysis*★ and will remember the mild and friendly fun he makes of Bruckner at this point:

"The orthodox critic has no right to complain of a shock to his habits of thought until he is confronted, not with an innovation, but with a stiff archaic pause on the dominant of B flat, the most conventional key that can be chosen for the second group of material. The stiffness is not accounted for by the fact that that group here begins in D flat instead; such evasions are as old as Cherubini's Overture to *Faniska*. And when Bruckner begins his second group and catechizes children with it in four-bar sequences ranging easily round the harmonic world, no wonder our musical Francis Jeffreys said (and in London continue to say) 'This will never do!' But this will have to do; for we are at the parting of the ways; and Bruckner has no theoretic labels with which to disguise his simplicity."

The first observation to make about this is that Tovey is right in suggesting that the orthodox critic might be startled by Bruckner's formal marking of time on these F major chords at the end of the first *tutti*. But they are most noticeable because in the context Bruckner has so far established they are unorthodox, the last thing we expect. On the other hand, they are natural enough, carried rhythmically by the general pulse; as with all things that combine naturalness with the unexpected, they are striking. In any case we remember them, whether we smile or not, which is what the composer wants. Now consider the continuation. Is the beginning of the second group in D flat really an "evasion"? An effect it has which no one can deny is that of making

★ Oxford University Press.

us remember all the more vividly those chords on the dominant of B flat. Try starting the next theme in B flat, and see how rapidly the impression of the previous four bars fades, becoming merely a formal gesture that has served its purpose. This is obvious enough, and there is no need to belabour the point. But it is important to Bruckner that the dominant of B flat should imprint itself on the mind; and a simple means of ensuring this is more efficacious than an involved one. He has his reasons, and they are not confined to a period of eight bars; they are concerned with the whole of this second group, which is about to have a long debate with itself as to whether it is to be in D flat or B flat. The average listener who neither knows nor cares what key the music is in must be assured that it is these very events that are, if he is enjoying the music, keeping his ear engaged, whether he realizes it or not. So here is the start of the second group, full of rustic charm yet not undignified, with two combined elements in the first phrase:

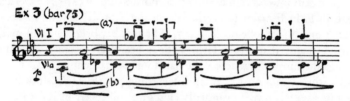

Because there can be no question of any counterstatement of the immensely broad opening, Bruckner has actually saved space, so that the second group can begin after 74 bars, as compared with 100 in No. 3. Of the two contrasting figures (a) and (b) in Ex. 3, the upper one, with its attractive bird-call, seems at first the more important, but it is the flowing counterpoint (b) that eventually exerts more influence. A new figure, more assertive, is soon heard:

I do not much mind if anyone cares to derive it from the inverted form of Ex. 2. From its initial D flat the tonality drifts through a series of dominants as far as E major (really F flat), returning to a suspended (6/4) form of D flat at bar 107. The A flat in the bass falls to F as a *crescendo* develops, and a *tutti* on Ex. 2 thunders out in B flat major.

Bruckner is beginning to show his argument. The *tutti* is checked on E flat (now the subdominant of B flat); at bar 131 there is a hush, and excited mystifications. Another *crescendo* brings about a resumption of the *tutti* in D flat! It results in a steep descent to *ppp* on a diminished seventh that cannot be convincingly resolved on to either D flat or B flat. Nothing but a unison F is left (bar 151). Is this going to be the dominant of B flat? We cannot tell as the strings rise chromatically. The doubts are grandly resolved by the brass—with chords of D flat followed at once by a German sixth in B flat, in which key Ex. 3 makes a gentle cadence, extended by quiet chromatic figures to what is clearly the end of the exposition. Without the orthodox critic's pain the whole process would have been impossible. It is a small price to pay.

The development commences in reflective mystery, the chromatic string figures alternating with a plaintive reference to Ex. 1. The key of B flat begins to sound like the dominant of E flat when there is a magical drift into foreign harmony, a chord that proves to be a German sixth in F. In F major (a bright key in the context) developments of Exx. 1 and 2 softly begin (bar 217). The tonality brightens still more, into A major (bar 219). Then with a beautiful *crescendo* Bruckner swings the music clean across the harmonic firmament to E flat minor and a stormy *tutti* on Ex. 2. An intervening *pianissimo* does not interrupt its sweep before it eventually closes magnificently in B flat major. Despite this *tutti* in E flat minor and B flat there is no sense of forestalling the recapitulation; the approach to E flat minor through A major makes sure of that. In the first movement of the Sixth Symphony Bruckner makes an astounding approach to his A major recapitulation from E flat, but that is another matter, to be considered in its context. It is interesting to compare, however, the situations at this juncture in the Third and Fourth symphonies.

It will be remembered that in No. 3, half-way through the development, the first theme was brought in on the full orchestra in the tonic key; the effect was disastrous because all momentum was thereby killed, an accident from which the movement as a whole never fully recovered. We may well imagine the fatal results that would have ensued in No. 4 if Bruckner had, at bar 253, suddenly delivered the horn theme of Ex. 1 *fortissimo* on the full band.* But he has learned his lesson, and bases the central passage of his development on the material that is by nature most active, namely Ex. 2. He therefore achieves his

* The rhythms and tempi of the two themes are not dissimilar, so the comparison is facilitated.

object of placing E flat and its dominant in the ear at a strategic moment without losing momentum. Indeed, momentum is positively increased by this *tutti*, and its last chord of B flat is given great impetus by the quickening and tightening of the harmony in the previous bar.

As the grand reverberations die away, Ex. 1 is heard high in the light vault of B flat major, and as if this key evokes distant memories and responses, there is a change to C sharp major, which is only our old friend D flat in disguise. The notation at once recognizes the fact and Ex. 1 is formed into a wonderful modulating chorale, perhaps the finest and most inspired passage in the whole of Bruckner up to this time. The scoring of this in the Gutmann edition of 1889 is a model of how to ruin glorious music. In the original the brass chorale is accompanied by a nobly striding counterpoint in the violas, strengthened by clarinets and bassoons. One could perhaps understand an editor or conductor suggesting that the addition of cellos might further support this line, which has the full-throated brass to contend with; it is not really necessary, but it would do no worse than slightly spoil the half-perceived perspective effect characteristic of Bruckner. But to turn it into a *pizzicato*, to add triplets rippling prettily up and down in the flutes and oboes, to make the horns play pulsating harmonies! Bruckner surely cannot have committed such a crime.

For the second time in the development, the tonality travels from one side of the universe to the other, this time from D flat to G major, where the chorale falls to rest. In G comes a new slow transformation of Ex. 3 (b), modulating with deep feeling round to the home dominant. The recapitulation opens with Ex. 1, now enriched in octaves and with a tranquil counterpoint on the flute. Muted violins are added in the 1889 publication, creating a sultry atmosphere where there should be sweet fresh air. At first the modulations are as before, but with new phrases on cellos answering the woodwind, and there is no *crescendo* this time (in the original score), so that the *tutti* breaks out suddenly. Bruckner did not forget the *crescendo*, and the late revision was not merely supplying a missing dynamic; in the original at the point where the *crescendo* began in the exposition, he marks the restatement *pp sempre*. Now the *tutti* changes its direction at the last minute; the massive formal half-close, instead of being on the dominant of B flat, is on that of A flat.

Again this "stiff archaic pause"* is responsible for a subtlety. In any sonata movement of such basic simplicity and clarity as this, to stand

* It is not, to be strictly accurate, a pause.

on the threshold of the subdominant at an advanced stage in the design
is to suggest that the end is not far away. A flat is the subdominant in
this case. It is too early to close into it, but the mere suggestion of it is
enough to render the restatement of the second group organically
active rather than merely static, symmetrical, and possibly redundant.
It now has some natural resistance to work against; it operates under
the shadow of a suggested impending *dénouement*, which its function
is to delay till the proper time. But it must do it with tact, for nothing
must disturb the majestic progress of this essentially calm movement;
there must be no tonal technicolor. So Ex. 3 enters in B major, which
bears exactly the same relationship to the dominant of A flat as, in the
exposition, did D flat to the dominant of B flat. B in this context is,
of course, really C flat. This time the continuation of Ex. 3 traces a
different series of keys; in the exposition it passed down a succession
of dominants, now it rises by minor thirds, from B (bar 437) to D
(bar 445), then to F (bar 459). The next stage should be A flat! But
we are not to be caught out. The purpose of this section is to avoid the
subdominant. Instead, with poetic, hesitating circumspection, Bruckner
slips back to the first region, B, now frankly written as C flat (bar 469),
which shows that after all it is not really a key, but only a flat sixth. It
falls to B flat, the home dominant, and a *crescendo* brings in the *tutti*
that appeared at the corresponding place in the exposition, but now in
the tonic. It is shortened, falls away into C minor (the first time we
have heard this key definitely stated, amazing in an E flat movement
of these dimensions), and the *coda* has begun.

Ex. 1 is combined with running woodwind figures that may or may
not be distantly related to similar earlier ones in the movement, or
even to Ex. 2—I can imagine one or two of our enthusiastic themati-
cists triumphantly dredging up this, for instance:*

Ex. 5 (bar 511)

Not that it matters much; it is not initiated in this form, and takes
many others. Through all this Bruckner keeps up an impressive rocking accompaniment, definitely grown from the string figuration of the
previous *tutti*. A shift to D flat prepares a powerful burst on G flat,

* But see Ex. 17 on p. 113!

rising to A flat (but not the subdominant, only supertonic in G flat). From A flat, with a return to *pianissimo*, the music rises in semitones, and Ex. 1 enters in a glowing E major at bar 533. When it slips into A flat major at bar 541 we know we are at last in the subdominant, and the end is in sight. With a perfect sense of architecture the last climax affirms the tonic, with Ex. 1 given a majestic *fortissimo* setting for the first time in the vast movement. True, it is only the first phrase of Ex. 1; but Bruckner has learned (certainly unconsciously) from the mistake of the Third, and knows that this phrase, played in this way any earlier in the piece, would have dangerously impeded momentum. Its function at the finish is (and I almost refrain from mentioning the fact) to stop the movement. This first movement is a masterpiece of serene grandeur, finer even than Tovey thought, and easily surpassing anything Bruckner had done before.

The *Andante* has something of the veiled funeral march about it, as if it were dreamt; sometimes we seem close to it, even involved, sometimes we seem to see it from so great a distance that it appears almost to stand still. It is hard to explain subjectively the uncannily poised nature of this movement, caught to perfection when Bruno Walter conducted it; some performances can be soporific, when the delicate and original atmosphere and the singularity of the structure are not exactly perceived. Impatience is always damaging to Bruckner's music—here it can be fatal. The point unfortunately has to be illustrated by yet another disagreement with the greatest of writers on music, Tovey. To quote him again:

"The defence of Bruckner, still necessary in this country, would defeat itself by attempting to claim that there is nothing helpless about the slow movement of the Romantic Symphony. . . . Bruckner's difficulty, this time a real inherent dilemma, in even his most perfect slow movements is, first, that his natural inability to vary the size of his phrases is aggravated by the slow tempo, and secondly, that the most effective means of relief is denied him by his conscientious objection to write anything so trivial and un-Wagnerian as a symmetrical tune. Consequently his all-important contrasting episode is as slow as his vast main theme. The result is curious: the thing that is oftenest repeated and always expanded, the vast main theme, is welcomed whenever it returns; while, as Johnson would have said, 'the attention retires' from even a single return of the episode . . . in the Romantic Symphony the difficulty is almost schematically exhibited by the structure of the episode, which consists of no less than seven phrases, all ending in full closes or half-closes, all four bars long except the last but one, and all given to the viola with a severely simple accompaniment of *pizzicato* chords in slow march time. There may, for all I know, be Brucknerites who consider this the finest thing in the symphony; and it so obviously 'will never do' that to criticize it on Jeffrey's lines will 'do' still less."

Luckily Bruckner does not now have to be defended in Britain so fiercely as when Tovey wrote that in the period between the wars. We no longer have to say, with him, "I forbear to quote the next two bars lest the enemy blaspheme". But it is still a pity to show the enemy cause for blasphemy where none exists. Tovey's criticism is more Jeffreyan than I think he knew, for it is based on an *a priori* principle such as he often and rightly deplored. It is his formula for the typical Bruckner slow movement (quoted on p. 35), and his assumption that there is an "episode".

In tonal symphonic music on the scale of Bruckner's we must always test the thematic organization against the tonal, to discover if a just equilibrium exists between the two elements, each of prime importance. Themes are always more easily noticed than tonalities; a theme's tonality is its condition, determining its feeling, or sense of direction, in relation to the whole scheme. The whole of the first part of the *Andante* of the Fourth begins and ends in C, and it contains three thematic ideas, all contributing to a total effect of quiescence. Here they are:

Ex 6
Andante, quasi allegretto
Vlns, Vlas, con sord

Ex. 7 (bar 25)

Ex. 8 (bar 51)

The first is a plain marching tune with a subdued accompaniment of muted strings. The tonic C minor is obscured but not banished when this leads to Ex. 7, a mysterious chorale of deep solemnity whose harmonic shifts are too constant for any new key to establish itself. Dying away, it is succeeded by the quietest idea of all, Ex. 8, a *cantilena* of violas, almost still, with the distant tread of remote *pizzicati*. Beginning in C minor, but dimly lit by gleams of other keys, it settles at last in C major, the first real close in the movement so far. This last is the theme Tovey describes as "the episode". In fact it is the final part of a *cortège*, viewed, if you like, from a very distant fixed point, so that its movement is scarcely perceptible. To take an astronomical analogy, the stars do not appear to move (relative to each other) in the sky because they are so distant. With precise measurement over a period of time, however, some do in fact show what is known as "proper motion"; it is very small, but it is detectable. It will be a long time before the position of Sirius in the sky is noticeably different, but it will be so. The vast opening section of this *Andante* also has its proper motion, for the C major in which it ends at bar 83 has a slight tendency to be the dominant of F minor. We need not be surprised at this, because in a minor key the tonic major is very likely to sound as if it might lead to the subdominant.

The change, through D flat to A flat, that follows this section shows at once the real effect of a clean change of key (bar 93). Starting in A flat, action now becomes apparent, and fragments of Ex. 6 are developed with new shapes, building a big climax that subsides on the home dominant in readiness for the restoration of the quiescence in C minor. If Bruckner were always a clumsy composer, he would now have a symmetrical recapitulation, and the attention would undoubtedly retire. There is indeed a restatement, but treated in a very individual manner; Bruckner now reverses normal sonata methods. The opening paragraph is certainly expository, but because it has only one tonal centre, it has no movement. Nevertheless, this does not preclude further activity of a developmental kind, for no sense of form has yet been achieved; the music has no alternative but to go on, and with contrasting action. This action creates tension, after which nothing can be exactly as it was before—so flat symmetry is out of the question. If the recapitulation is not to be static, it must therefore move just a little more than the "exposition", and so it does. Ex. 6 enters as before in C minor, the chorale is omitted (since it would give the impression of flat symmetry at the very moment when variance is required), and Ex. 8 follows, not beginning in C minor, but in D minor, ending in the major at bar 186. So the composer's surprising solution has been to deal with the necessary restatement as if it were a primitive kind of sonata exposition; its end left open, a *coda* grows perforce. Bruckner moves gravely back to C minor and on the main theme slowly piles up a tremendous mass of tone before letting it die impressively away with oblique references to Ex. 7 and Ex. 8. This *coda* is what he has all the time been aiming at, and it would have been impossible if the "exposition" had moved tonally, leaving the recapitulation to remain static.

Such a scheme as this is true to itself, and has no precedent or successor in Bruckner's or anybody else's work. It can be adversely criticized only by the stratagem of omitting vital factors from consideration, or failing to observe them. In either case the criticism amounts to special pleading for its own limitations. If, for lack of patience or any other necessary condition, we miss the essential atmosphere of the music, how can we be expected to analyse it correctly? Tovey is almost always reliable in these matters, which is why it is a pity to have to argue with him rather than with the kind of unimaginative mass of pedantic prejudices that so often was the just target of his wit.

The next movement is the first great Scherzo by Bruckner. His favourite mixed rhythm dominates it:

Ex. 9
Bewegt

At such a quick tempo this rhythm is often inaccurately played, and the failure of concentration that causes this also reduces the energy (and consequently the significance) of the music. The key is B flat major, and the opening is a strong and formal-seeming accumulation of dissonant harmony on a tonic pedal, the *crescendo* running into a wonderful shock:

Ex. 10 (bar 27)

The trumpets thrillingly answer the challenges with tonic and dominant, but the reaction is pensive, a subtly transformed version of Ex. 10:

Ex. 11 (bar 35)

This flows into quietly running triplets derived from Ex. 10 (a); then Ex. 9 settles purposefully down to build a spacious but terse *crescendo* to a blaze of fanfares in F major. It completes the exposition. The development, with reduced tempo, drops into a mysterious G flat, at first answering the inversion of Ex. 9 with the questioning Ex. 11 (a). G flat becomes A; the same thing happens, with Ex. 9 imaginatively overlapping its own inversion in soft horn and trumpet. Ex. 11 (a) and its inversion now assume control, soon introspectively reaching E minor, the remotest possible key from the original tonic B flat. It becomes major (bar 120), then cellos sing warmly through E flat and thence to the home dominant. The tension rises and the recapitulation starts at bar 163; it contains delicate tonal changes that make all the difference to its inner life (compare bar 195 *et seq.* with Ex. 11, and bars 206–11 with 46–51). The scoring, too, is often finely altered.

The Trio is the simplest Bruckner wrote; nothing could be more amiably rustic than its tune:

Ex 12

But nothing could be less rustic (or more amiable) than the exquisitely judged tonal side-slips that distinguish its second half. In the original version the Scherzo is repeated in full; in the 1889 publication there is a cut from the bar before Ex. 10 (so that the *crescendo* is abruptly cut off) to the low G flat at the start of the development. Tovey finds this "extremely effective", but I must confess deafness to the virtues of following an abortive *crescendo* on a tonic pedal by a reflective development section in a different tempo. Nor do I much care for the cautious *diminuendo* that leads to the Trio in this version; the latter seems the more memorable for the strong contrast of the original.

In the Finale, problems loom again. The Third Symphony showed Bruckner groping after a new type of finale; the difficulty was not only one of scale and proportion. In classical symphonic music the artistic problem has always been to find a last movement that will somehow arise naturally from the combined effect of the first three, that will be accurately informed by the resultant of three (or sometimes two) different forces. Many romantic composers, mistakenly claiming Beethoven as mentor, have taken the easy way out of this profoundly taxing problem by substituting facile emotional progression for organic growth, so that the finale can seem to be the obvious dramatic conclusion, triumphal or despairing as the case may be (it is *always* one or the other with such composers!). The kind of finale Bruckner is aiming at in the Third and Fourth symphonies is still only dimly perceived, and it is very different in nature from everything else that was being done by others at the time; I do not think it has been achieved since, if indeed it has even been attempted. Not being a very articulate or consciously analytical man, Bruckner probably never tried to explain his aims to himself, except in purely emotional and religious terms; nevertheless we can see in his work the stages by which his instinct crept nearer its goal.

The energy of the classical finale is a resultant force. The rhetoric of a romantic finale is an emotional and sometimes brainless reaction. Both are after-effects; they are not necessarily summings-up, but they are the conclusive upshot of previous stimuli. The type of Bruckner finale we are discussing is neither resultant nor reaction; nor is it a summing-up. It is not an after-effect, nor any kind of conclusion. The immense climaxes that end the Fifth and Eighth symphonies may seem to render these statements absurd. Such climaxes, however, far from being driven by the accumulated energy of a vividly muscular process (as in the classical symphony) or by the warring of emotive

elements (as in the purely romantic work), are rather the final intensi-
fication of an essence. A Bruckner symphony is, so to speak, an
archeological "dig". The first three movements are like layers removed,
revealing the city below, the finale. Or they may be regarded as layers
of consciousness, as it were peeled away to show their origins, if such a
thing were possible. Bruckner's finale is intended (unconsciously—
and how else could it be?) to form the bedrock of the symphony,
its background contemplated, its essence crystallized, the sky through
which the earth moves—choose what metaphor you like. Such a
phenomenon is inevitable, because the first three movements do not
generate the kind of energy that propels a classical finale, or delineate
the sort of emotional drama that precipitates a romantic catharsis. This
is the basic reason why, as Tovey puts it, "you must not expect Bruckner
to make a finale 'go' like a classical finale". Equally, we must not expect
him to provide impassioned rhodomontade or theatrical fireworks.

So remarkable a concept could not easily be grasped by the composer; failures were as inevitable as the search itself. In the case of the
Third Symphony the imperfections of the previous movements were
an added complication; the foundations on which they rested were in
part shifting sands, uncovered in the Finale. No such serious inequalities
undermine the first three movements of the Fourth, and the chances of
finding solid rock in the Finale are much higher. But Bruckner's skill
in this deepest kind of excavating is not yet fully developed. In the
finales of both Third and Fourth, however, we can see a sign that he is
aware of the nature of the problem, even though he has not yet felt
it clearly enough to attack it from the right quarter. Both these movements begin with a massive paragraph that ends in the tonic key. The
finales of the Third, Fourth, Fifth, Sixth, and Eighth symphonies all
begin with monolithic statements of this kind, ending either in the tonic
or on the home dominant. The absolute character of these movements
is laid plainly down at the outset. The Finale of No. 4 opens impressively
in B flat minor with the object of facing slowly in the tonic direction
after the key of the Scherzo. Bellatrix and Betelgeuse gleam low in
the East as a mysterious configuration climbs clear of the horizon:

Ex 13

More stars peep from the dusky sky. Excitement grows as Orion's belt and sword (the rhythm of the Scherzo) dimly appear. At last Orion himself stands awesome, brilliant across black space, splendid, complete:

E flat is established, and although D minor storm clouds pass across the constellation, the bright stars reappear. A feature of the cloud is this shape:

As we return towards E flat the rhythm of Ex. 1 from the first movement is heard (trombones, bar 63). A grand climax dies away in E flat major after Ex. 1 has plainly emerged in the horns. The music has not moved; instead it has made the conditions for a contemplative process. A thoughtful idea in C minor follows in slower tempo:

With a change to the major naïvety prevails. We will not, like Tovey, forbear to quote the second two bars of this theme, and will, moreover, join the enemy in blaspheming heartily. Alas, this is not merely naïvety—it is triviality. For twenty-five years I have tried to persuade myself that there must be something else, some redeeming subtlety behind this crackjaw platitude; at last, compelled to go into print, I must admit ignominious defeat:

It is all very well to say, as do romantic Brucknerites, that much of the fascination of this composer is due to his ability to contrast the sublime and the bucolic, the Austrian mountains and the simple peasants, etc., etc. It is sometimes true, though I suspect that in many cases the observation is prompted by a sentimental love of the picturesque, for it rarely discriminates between cases like this one and more successful examples such as can be found elsewhere in Bruckner. When Mahler appears deliberately to cultivate the banal we often hear the same argument, frequently indiscriminate. Like Bruckner, Mahler is not always the master of difficulties of this kind, and advocates would do him more service by trying to find out where and why this is so. The successes are then so much more impressive.

The fault here must certainly lie not only in the poor little theme itself, but in the placing of it. Bruckner might have got away with it, and with some humour, at the tail end of a section, but its discovery immediately after the grave Ex. 16 has the effect of an empty cigarette packet picked up in Pompeii. It is surprising that Tovey did not reserve his strictures for this part of the symphony. The continuation has charm,

but now the fussy two-bar periods become tiresome. We must accept that this Finale is not going to move in the conventional sense of the word, that in fact a great static quality is its positive attribute; but there is movement of a vast and quiescent kind that Bruckner has now temporarily lost. Orion, hitherto majestic in the sky, seems to be catching flies.

D

From the C major at bar 105, Bruckner toddles to two more recitations of the nursery rhyme, sitting down in A flat (bar 125) and in F (bar 139). F turns out to be the dominant of B flat, and all this nonsense is abruptly swept aside by a magnificent *tutti*, beginning in B flat minor (bar 155). If only the composer had allowed Ex. 16 to flow out into the broad paragraph it promised to be, how inevitable would this *tutti* have seemed! A new theme on the brass strides in combination with Ex. 15 and the *tutti* moves authoritatively to the dominant of B flat. Instead of the expected resolution, however, G flat intervenes with a reflective and highly original treatment of Ex. 15 with more new figures. G flat being only a flat sixth, it is not long before B flat drifts back, this time tranquilly in the major.

So ends the first stage of the movement. Despite the lapse between bars 105 and 155, the proportions are now becoming apparent. Imagine the whole so far, those fifty bars filled out with a cogent paragraph of great seriousness and beauty based on Ex. 16; we would have a mighty expository passage of ample variety and irreproachable grandeur, informed with a tremendous slowness of motion in travelling from E flat to B flat via C minor. It is not the progression of sonata music, but is more like a huge slow swing round part of a tonal orbit, different themes in different keys taking their places like the various constellations along the line of the ecliptic. In the Finale of the Eighth Symphony Bruckner found a wonderful way of gradually swinging back again from this point, not dissimilar from his method in the first movement of the Seventh. Here, however, his touch is far less sure, because he has not yet shaken off the confusing influence of sonata. The origins of Ex. 17 may well lie in a nervous feeling that the supposed sonata movement needed speeding up at that moment, Bruckner not yet understanding that he was composing something utterly strange; instead he stopped the real motion.

The tempo of the opening comes back, and Ex. 13, inverted, begins to rise from key to key. This is a beautiful passage, and a gradual *crescendo* mounts towards C sharp minor, then A major, a new melody trying to form in the woodwind, exquisitely adorned by *pizzicati*. But instead of new and rich developments, Ex. 17 breaks in loudly on the brass in G flat major, answered squarely by the strings in G sharp minor (only a supertonic reply despite the notation). Alas— sabotage again. The promising flow is stemmed; once more the music shuffles along two bars at a time, with desultory treatment of Exx. 17 and 18, and soon peters out on the dominant of F (bar 268). In F minor

Ex. 16 tries to remedy the situation. But it now has no roots, and no sense of being carried by a momentum larger than its own. So it tends to wander in ever-tiring sequences, first of two bars, then of one, and finally stagnating on the dominant of A (bar 291).

Such stagnation, however, can only arouse expectation. Something must happen, because obviously at this stage in the piece it cannot possibly be nothing. So there is almost an air of tension, and it is shattered by a sudden *fortissimo* in C, Ex. 13 rising by semitones in a *tutti* even grander than the previous one. Again this might have been the culmination of a fine stretch of development from bar 203; instead it has to be a rescue operation. But for the time being disappointments are forgotten in an expanse of stormy music of masterly authority. The pitch rises from C to D flat, D, E flat, E and then, as the gigantic rhythm broadens still more, by whole tones through F sharp to A flat as Ex. 13 expands into the full Ex. 14. It bursts the bounds of A flat, crashing over into alien harmony as it falls steeply away into D major (bar 339) in what may be termed a polar modulation of great power, and one of the few moments in this symphony that faintly recall Wagner.

Now follows an extraordinary passage. Everything is in fragments. The D major fades into a strange augmentation of Ex. 15, apparently on the dominant of A, but leading to a mysterious inversion of Ex. 14 in D minor with a pulsating accompaniment. Its last chord, instead of being D minor, is B flat, which is not at once recognizable as the home dominant. Not much could be more remote than E flat. But over a long B flat drum roll, scraps of Ex. 14, some of them weirdly miniature, joined by echoes of the Scherzo, collect themselves together, seeming to huddle expectantly on what is now decidedly the dominant of E flat.

Bruckner obviously sees this fantastically original inspiration as a tense preparation for a sonata restatement, for in the original version he follows it at once with Ex. 14 in E flat on the full orchestra. But something is seriously wrong. The fragmented passage feels very much like an aftermath of the previous *tutti*, not like a preparation, and the statement of Ex. 14 in E flat at bar 383 lacks the momentum that ought to be behind a recapitulation. It seems like an afterthought, or perhaps an appendix to the previous *tutti*. Conviction leaves it as it labours its way to the dominant of F sharp, then falls silent. Something *is* wrong. What?

As in the earlier unconvincing parts of this movement, the mistake is rooted in the confusion between sonata and what Bruckner is groping after. It is not that recapitulation should be out of the question—any large form is bound to need recapitulatory elements at some time or other. The error lies in the composer's not having consistently felt the larger momentum that renders sonata strategy irrelevant. Consequently some passages are of the wrong kind (Ex. 17 *et seq.*) and some turn up in the wrong places (the fragmented section, bars 339–82). This last would have been perfectly deployed as a dissolving element before matters are finally gathered together in a great *coda*. Imagine it (or something like it) preceding bar 477.

Movements like this can arouse one's sympathy for Bruckner's friends who wanted to help him get things right. But how could they be expected, so near to the event, to see what he was really trying to do? At this stage he can have had little idea himself, and would certainly have been incapable of explaining to anyone. It is obvious that the *tutti* at bar 383 is both laboured and redundant. But chopping it out is no remedy, which is what happens in the 1889 publication. In the original it is followed by Ex. 16 in F sharp minor, on whose dominant it breaks off; in the "revision", with the *tutti* cut out, Ex. 16 enters in D minor immediately after the fragmented passage, the whole trend of which has been to modulate away from D minor to the home dominant. A drunken surgeon attending to a lame centipede could scarcely get into a worse muddle.

But Bruckner himself does not improve matters when Ex. 17 enters in D major at bar 431 (we are now back with the original version). Ex. 18 follows; this time the succession of tonalities is not the same, but there is little to be done about the two-bar merry-go-round. At bar 449 there is an attempt to cover the stiffness of Ex. 17 with rich lyricism, but it makes no difference. Then the mood changes to solemnity as the rhythm of the first bar of Ex. 17 is combined with Ex. 15, and a *crescendo* rises. There is a hush, and a genuinely impressive fall to the home dominant.

The *coda* is, after all this, one of Bruckner's greatest culminative passages. It would be greater still had it arisen from the kind of process he was later to master. But though it must begin with little tension to set it off, it is nevertheless superlatively fine music. Listening to it is like walking through a mighty cathedral, as Ex. 13 is intoned with wonderful hushed deliberation. A horn forms a long, fine line of melody, trumpets sound from on high. Then the harmonies begin gloriously to change as the final *crescendo* swells. The end is magnificently conclusive, and one is briefly convinced that, after all, the Finale must have been a masterpiece.*

* In the most recent publication of the Bruckner Society, edited by Leopold Nowak, an amendment has been made to the final *tutti*, giving the main figure of the first movement to the horns. This is based on a manuscript found in New York and represents Bruckner's own final wishes—but there is, I think, still a strong artistic case to be made for the restraint of the original (as shown in Haas's edition), in which the rhythm of the theme is present, but not its actual notes.

CHAPTER VI

SYMPHONY NO. 5, IN B FLAT MAJOR

Soon after finishing the first draft of No. 4, Bruckner began
work on the Fifth, starting with the *Adagio* in February, 1875. His
circumstances were difficult; he had very little money—only the fees
from his ill-paid teaching at the Konservatorium in Vienna—and his
work was not arousing much interest. He was not at home in the
sophisticated capital and was regretting having moved from Linz,
where he had been happy in a sympathetic atmosphere. Herbeck had
found him a post as piano tutor at a seminary for women teachers,
but he was victimized after two students had complained that he had
insulted them. Redlich is probably right in suggesting that "it seems
likely that his rough peasant dialect and rural manner had caused a
regrettable misunderstanding",* but the press did not interpret it in
that way. Bruckner's innocence appears to have been proved, but not
before he had suffered much. He was consigned to the men's section
with a lower salary, and soon afterwards the job was abolished. He
was forced to borrow money, and was unsuccessfully looking for
work abroad. He wrote to Moritz von Mayfeld, "My life has lost all
joy and enthusiasm—and all for nothing. How I wish I could go back
to my old post!" All these dismal facts perhaps give added poignancy
to the D minor oboe theme in the *Adagio* of the Fifth, the first part of
the work to be written.

The whole symphony was done by May 1876. He retouched it in
1878, but not again after that, and its first publication was supervised
by Franz Schalk during the composer's last illness in 1896. Schalk's
wholesale re-orchestration of the work, his ruinous truncation of the
Finale, and his introduction of an extra brass band at the end are now
history and need not be detailed here; it will be difficult enough to
confine an analysis of the authentic score of this colossal symphony to a
single chapter. It must be said, however, that since Bruckner is known
not to have approved (or perhaps even seen) Schalk's score, and since
the alterations are all very similar to those made in some of the
other symphonies, we should be very suspicious of claims that "the
Master gave his blessing", etc., etc., in those parallel cases. Nearly all

* *Bruckner and Mahler* (J. M. Dent).

such changes are totally uncharacteristic of Bruckner; this should be the real test.

Apart from the unfinished Ninth, No. 5 was the only one of Bruckner's symphonies of which he never heard a note performed. Schalk conducted it in Graz in 1894, but Bruckner was too ill to attend—just as well for him, perhaps, though he would in any case have been unlikely to put his foot down over the matter of the alterations. He had hopes that Schalk would give a performance in Vienna, but this did not happen. Ferdinand Loewe did so two years after the composer's death. If Bruckner could have heard a fine and successful performance of his own score of this, one of his very greatest works, it might have made all the difference to his confidence in later years. Who knows—had he been spared the futile revisions of the first three symphonies near the end of his life, he might have finished the Ninth.

It has often been noted that this is the only Bruckner symphony to begin with a slow introduction. The obvious reason for this is Bruckner's normal slow pace. A less obvious reason is that all the other symphonies do have brief introductions. In Nos. 4, 7, 8 and 9 these preambles are slower than slow—they are tempo-less *tremolandi*, spanning the space between silence and Bruckner. Nos. 1, 2, 3, 6 and the posthumous D minor symphony begin against rhythmic backgrounds that are not less introductory because they set a tempo. It is Bruckner's nature to begin with an intake of breath; whatever caused his personal diffidence also brought about the magical beginnings of most of his symphonies. The last movement of No. "o" has a recurring slow introduction, but it is more decorative than organic. That which opens the Fifth is made to spread its influence over the whole symphony, tonally and thematically. It would be fascinating to know the composer's mental processes during the formation of this symphony. We do know that he began with the *Adagio* in D minor, but not how clearly he was conceiving it as part of a work in B flat major. Whatever the truth, there can be no doubt that the beginning of the work could well have been (and very nearly is) an introduction to a symphony in D minor. In that case it is likely the *Adagio* and Scherzo would have been in different keys; both are in D minor. So it is probable that B flat was predetermined. Perhaps it was mere depression that made him write first the bleak opening of the slow movement.

The first movement of the Fifth Symphony is an altogether singular piece. There is something fascinatingly introductory about the whole of it, in relation to the rest of the symphony. This is caused by the fact that it is in reality a search for a tonality; it is one of those movements that presents a very odd appearance if we persist in looking at it purely as sonata form, but as soon as we use our ears rather than our eyes the entire process is clear and the piece seems only half the length. Sonata is plainly its ancestor, but is no more than a background to events. As always with Bruckner, it is wise to trace these events from point to point, and see where they lead. First, noble and mysterious counterpoint grows in B flat major over an *ostinato*:

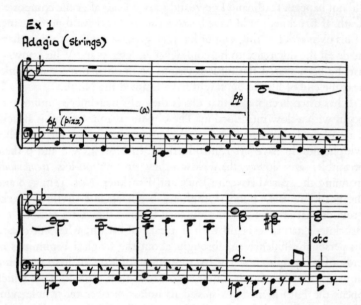

Inflexions of the minor darken the music as it hesitates on the dominant. Silence—then a great burst of tone on G flat major:

Again silence, and now a blaze of brass, like a mighty organ, with another stunning change of harmony, into A major (with a G natural that makes it sound like the dominant of D):

Ex 3 (bar 18)

No symphony ever opened like this. Another silence, and with the added force of the timpani Ex. 2 is thundered forth on B flat major. As before it ceases abruptly, and again the brass deliver the paean of Ex. 3, now on the dominant of A. Silence.

This magnificent and unique opening, with its great blocks of sound confronting each other on different harmonic pedestals, separated by open spaces, has already set up a vast momentum, slower than Bruckner had hitherto conceived. The silences should not really be such, for Bruckner certainly has in his mind's ear an immensely resonant cathedral acoustic. Such music as this can be ruined by the dryness of modern concert halls. Now comes another change. The previous dominant of A is confirmed (the first time we have been granted an expected tonality), but there is a new tempo, *Allegro*. The bass of Ex. 3 is now informed with quiet energy, there is a *crescendo*, and the orchestra seems like an expectant crowd as the A pedal becomes itself a dominant. The apex of this passage is an abrupt return to *adagio* and a massive expansion of Ex. 3 on the dominant of D, a sound of extraordinary power and depth.

So it sounds as if D is the goal, despite the opening in B flat. The high A dies away into the vault, and drops to D. The tempo changes back to *allegro*. But the D is made part of a B flat major chord, changing to minor as a new theme forms beneath:

Ex. 4 (bar 55)

The previous appearances of B flat at the beginning and at bar 23 have not been sufficiently prominent to give security to this B flat minor after the tremendous preparation for D, and it proves to be a characteristic of this movement that whenever B flat is not tonally on firm ground it tries to establish itself by turning to the minor. This gives the whole movement a minorish quality, though the official key is major. Confirming the insecurity of B flat, Ex. 4 at once goes to C sharp minor (really D flat minor). A new figure attaches itself, immediately undergoing transformations:

Such continuous thematic mutation is another typical trait of this symphony. Meanwhile the tonalities are slipping downwards with an increasing sense of bewilderment, reflected by a *crescendo*. The dominant of B flat minor is reached at the last moment and Ex. 4 follows in a defiant *fortissimo*. Still the key is far from fixed, and the *tutti* falls away with B flat now strangely and somewhat affrightedly behaving as dominant of E flat. Energy leaves the music, and its ripples die out. B flat is by no means a tonic yet, and has gone too far towards its subdominant for its own safety. The tendency has to be offset by a move in the opposite direction. In F minor a hesitant new *pizzicato* idea slowly assembles itself:

It is a tentative F minor, and even more so when sustained phrases quietly join the *pizzicato*. The atmosphere is mysterious and remote,

Ex 7 (bar 109)

similar to that of Ex. 8 in the Fourth Symphony (see p. 91), and movement is reduced to a minimum although there is no actual change of tempo. The burst of *allegro* energy that has passed is no more than a surface agitation above a vast slow current measured by the introduction. There is a slight flicker as a hint of D minor seems to touch ancient instincts (bar 125), but it is nothing, and the music's face is impassive as it turns away to D flat. Around this key soft woodwind figures hover above long and beautiful suspensions in the horns. But they turn eventually back to the dominant of F and, sphinx-like, Ex. 6–7 resumes. Now there is a rise in feeling as the key returns to F minor, on the dominant of which the music once more hesitates. Another new theme appears, but in D flat, warmer and more active:

Ex 8 (bar 161)

Woodwind

Notice the bass:

Ex 9 (bar 161)

With great dignity and easy carriage Ex. 8 swings forward to a D flat major *fortissimo* on the rhythm but not the shape of Ex. 9 (bar 177). Another stride finds A major (bar 181). It is the dominant of D, and with a sudden *piano* the music begins to move purposefully in D minor. Is this, after all, the real direction? But no—D minor is edged aside in a *crescendo* that culminates in a powerful unison theme, strongly rhythmic:

Ex. 10 (bar 199)

This sounds and behaves like a new idea (which it is) but it evolves directly from the diminished rhythm of Ex. 9. It also hammers at first at B flat but then turns its attention to G flat, on a chord of which a climax insists. We could, even now, be going to B flat, for the G flat is plainly a Neapolitan flat sixth. It would be a simple progression, and it looks almost inevitable:

Ex. 11

But instead there is a chord of D major, instituting the marvellous transformation of the chord of F major from a dominant in bar 209 to a tonic in bar 221. Examine this passage with great care; it is one of Bruckner's most beautiful miracles. Notice also that Ex. 9 has undergone yet another metamorphosis. So we reach the first full close, after 224 bars, and it is in F major. Our *routiniers* will of course say that this is only the proper dominant at the end of a sonata exposition. True, and we have also now heard all the themes. But what an astounding journey if we understand the real nature of the terrain it has traversed.

The movement has not yet succeeded in fixing a tonic, and must continue, for F major is but a brief resting place. The tonality moves quietly out of the magic circle of F, hovers on a chord of E major, and the music seems to stop and look round. Perhaps an approach can be made from a new direction; try a key that has not been heard before. So the *Adagio* returns, now in C major, and the slow counterpoint of the opening is played softly on horns with the *ostinato* below. It evokes Ex. 2, still in C major. Ex. 4 enters questioningly, *allegro*, in C minor. More doubtfully, the *Adagio* begins again in the strings, at first in the subdominant of C minor, but brightening slowly. The *ostinato* becomes seraphic as the woodwind take it up; the strings climb to the heights. The direction is E flat major, and there is no more radiant moment in the whole of Bruckner. Again Ex. 2 is the culmination. It breaks in on B flat, which sounds like the dominant of E flat; but the *arpeggio* is of B flat minor, with the instant effect of banishing the serene E flat. But B flat tonality is asserted, and the *allegro* starts again with Ex. 4. The theme is in canon with its own inversion; this creates another tonal disturbance, and the last two notes ask agitated questions.

The answer is a massive delivery by the full orchestra of the canon by inversion, launching a developing *tutti* of such formidable majesty as is scarcely to be found outside Beethoven's Ninth Symphony. Although there are passages of quiet, the whole process that follows has the force of an indivisible *tutti*, and its general aim is towards the establishment of B flat as a real key. Ex. 4 is combined with many versions of itself in many ways and at bar 283 is joined by the mighty Ex. 2. At intervals there is an insistence on B flat, each time stronger; the first is at bar 287, the second at bar 303, after a mysterious hush, with a new and powerful figure, at first on horns:

Ex 12 (bar 303)

At least it seems new, but it is in fact naturally thrown off by Ex. 2, and it infuses immense energy as it accelerates into notes of half the value with another drop to *pianissimo*. Now we are definitely on the dominant of B flat. The storm breaks afresh with huge descending lightning strokes (now the connection between Ex. 2 and Ex. 12 is absolutely clear). B flat topples over into G minor (bar 323), and is dramatically interrupted by the still small voice of Ex. 6, in distant solemn harmony on horns, *in D minor*. Trombones join the horns as the harmony turns unexpectedly into D flat. The whole orchestra then batters in fury at the door of B flat with Ex. 12 reduced to plain octave Fs. Again the strange quiet undermining influence of Ex. 6— this time from the remote distance of A minor; it shifts its tonality perplexedly, and it is as if something totally different were happening in another world. B flat seems lost and forgotten. Suddenly the brass blaze out with Ex. 3—in D? No, in B major, then A flat minor. The effect is electrifying, but B flat is obliterated by these alien tonalities.

There is nothing to do but try to gather the remnants of the shattered army, and quietly but determinedly a *crescendo* is built on the quickened bass of Ex. 3, on the dominant of B flat, in the manner of the passage in the introduction at bar 31. It is a multitudinous, defiantly repetitive *crescendo*, and marches into Ex. 4 in B flat minor. So we have at last reached B flat, and, moreover, with the only sustained dominant preparation so far in the movement. But it is a very different arrival from that anticipated, and although B flat is stronger than hitherto, it is still far from being an undisputed tonic. Inevitably its grip loosens as other keys, D flat, C, E flat, overrun it again. There is a puzzled halt on the dominant of G. In making use of such terms as these to describe the tendencies of the music, I hope I shall not be misunderstood: it must not be supposed, for instance, that it is Bruckner who is puzzled. In the Third Symphony and the Finale of No. 4 he is often so; here he is the master.

Now we have entered a crucial confluence in the movement. It will be remembered that in the Finale of No. 4 the *tutti* beginning at bar 383 was inadvertently made to seem like a redundant aftermath of a previous larger *tutti* because Bruckner, confusing his instinctive purposes with those of sonata, had almost arbitrarily introduced an official recapitulation. In the grand design we are now considering he masters the effect organically. The passage starting at bar 347, building a *crescendo* on the dominant of B flat and rising to the main theme in B flat minor at bar 363, with subsequent tonal instability and a halt at bar 380, is indeed the aftermath (rather than the climax) of the gigantic development so dramatically interrupted by the horns at bar 325. Bruckner is now achieving a marvellous interpenetration of streams. The soft incursion of Ex. 6 at bar 325 begins a process of infiltration, resulting in the breaking up of the continuous and seemingly irresistible force that was possessing the music. It takes the conviction out of the last massive attempt of this force to set up B flat, an artistic stroke with a purpose (as opposed to the embarrassing redundancy caused at bar 383 in the last movement of the Fourth).

The reason is that it is still too soon to establish B flat beyond all doubt. The movement is not only searching for a secure tonic, it is evolving a form with proportions and symmetries that cannot be truncated. In fact the two prime elements (the quest for a firm tonic and the creation of balanced structure) are organically interrelated. If there had not been this interpolation of Ex. 6, and if the *tutti* had been allowed to storm its way without hindrance to a climax in B flat (major or minor), the tonic would still not have been fully secured because the great slow momentum of the whole would have been forgotten in the excitement—and the safety of a tonic is always fundamentally a matter of momentum. The rider is safe only if the momentum of the horse is controlled. Bruckner has not forgotten this.

He knows that matter so prominent as Ex. 6 and its consequences (i.e., the whole complex from bar 101 to 223) cannot be subsequently ignored and, moreover, that its motion is basic to the design, the motion that has to be preserved whatever storms may lash the surface. But if it is to be recapitulated in any form, it must have a new function connected with the tonal development; while it creates thematic symmetry it must also help to control the inner growth of the music. So the next entrance of Ex. 6 (at bar 381) is in G minor, not far away from B flat major, and we may as well notice how Bruckner avoids the recapitulation of his "second subject" in the tonic. Ex. 6 has entered in stages, causing the great storm to vanish in bursts; again it takes calm, abstracted possession. There are few more profound or original large-scale incidents in symphonic music.

The first appearance of Ex. 6 in F minor at bar 101 was corrective to a tendency of B flat to slip down to its own subdominant. Now in G minor (with Ex. 7) it is preparing the ground on which a conclusive establishment of B flat can be raised. With the mysterious detachment that is its fascination it leads eventually to Ex. 8, now in E flat, the home subdominant, and the warm blood begins to circulate once more. This is the proper place to feel subdominant leanings, towards the end. As before, the bass of Ex. 8 generates Ex. 10; this time the music pulls back abruptly on the dominant of G minor. There is a pause, and then we hear the quiet throb of Ex. 1 (a) (in *allegro* tempo) in B flat minor, which immediately sounds like a tonic as Ex. 4 piles itself over the *ostinato*. Soft questions are asked on the dominant (are we really getting there at last?), answered in the affirmative by the full orchestra (bar 477). The theme is repeated, inverted, in F sharp minor, but there is now no argument, only a sudden hush and an invincible *crescendo* to a serenely formal peroration in B flat major, the first time we have properly heard the tonic major since the music began. And so ends this wonderful movement. It is always the Finale of this symphony that gets the publicity, as they say, and the first movement is much neglected by commentators. But it is one of the subtlest and most powerful of Bruckner's creations. It has not been possible to go into its fascinating textural details, and I hope the reader will find endless pleasure in discovering the myriad ways in which the themes are combined with themselves and each other (especially Ex. 2 and Ex. 4). Bruckner's counterpoint is naïve, but it is enormously imaginative and always amazingly clear; together with his skill in transforming themes it constitutes, so to speak, the movement's muscles by which it traverses its tonal territories with such mastery.

After the complexities of the first movement, the *Adagio* shows a broad and essentially simple outline, and it conforms almost exactly to Tovey's formula. Like most of Bruckner's slow movements, it has intricate inner detail, especially in the cross-rhythms which characterize the parts based on the main theme. It begins austerely, with quiet *pizzicati*:

This adumbrates the theme itself, on the oboe, at first making a disguised unison with Ex. 13:

It is like a bleak chorale prelude. The melody brightens towards F major, then droops away (bar 13). Falling sevenths are prominent in it; they dominate large stretches of the movement:

The last example ends on the dominant of F minor, but the strings, with warmer harmonies and more elaborate cross-rhythms, continue in C, then move towards B flat minor, around which is woven a beautiful chain of falling sevenths, threaded by light quavers in the violins. It all comes to rest on a chord of F major that still feels like the dominant of B flat rather than a key in its own right. But instead of B flat major or minor, however, there comes one of the world's great melodies, in a noble C major:

Ex 16 (bar 31)

A curious detail is that we first hear this theme in a modified form, simply because the violins cannot go below G; the second phrase (bar 35) shows the shape from which it never subsequently deviates. It is finely extended and contrapuntally developed in a very spacious paragraph, during which this figure should be noted:

Ex. 17 (bar 45)

The music floats through various harmonic regions, returning faithfully to C major twice—at bar 55 and at the climax with a 6/4 chord at bar 65. But C major is not clinched and a soft A major intervenes (bar 67). This proves to be the dominant of D minor when the first subject returns in the tonic, enveloped in flowing violin phrases. The falling sevenths become salient as modulations are gravely unfolded (these sevenths here and elsewhere in Bruckner have evoked comparisons with Elgar, but I find nothing in common between Elgar's splendiferous use of this interval and Bruckner's solemn simplicity of mind). Soon a *fortissimo* breaks out and tension mounts, becoming surprisingly explosive as *pp* and *ff* alternate in half-bars. Needless to say, the theme goes through a number of free inversions, and the falling-seventh figure is still identifiable even when it becomes rising sixths. The air is full of tragedy during this passage. It is cut off, and despondent fragments wander through a tonal limbo. They seem to be groping for E flat, but what appears to be a dominant seventh of E flat is magically interpreted as a German sixth in D major, in which key Ex. 16 returns with wonderful consolatory effect.

It flows through new modulations, again reaching an earnest and beautiful climax, which now leaves the music suspended on the home dominant, whence it descends by way of a long sequential treatment of Ex. 17 during which all colour and warmth drains slowly from the music. Unsympathetically performed, this passage can have unendurable *longueurs*; perfectly controlled, with a *diminuendo* such as may admittedly be achieved only with the finest orchestras, it can create an unforgettable atmosphere. For wise advice on the performance of this symphony, incidentally, I would commend an article *A Performer's Rights* by Stanley Pope in the 1963 issue of *Chord and Discord*;* this conductor has himself demonstrated on many occasions how to manage to perfection such passages in Bruckner.

At length the main theme comes back in D minor, accompanied by elaborate but chaste string ornamentation, mounting in Bruckner's inimitable and awe-inspiring way from climax to climax. The whole paragraph is like the nave of some great severe cathedral, far more Gothic than Baroque, with fine dark avenues of arches (the violin figuration) and mighty shafts (the descending sevenths). But it does not, like some other such passages in Bruckner's slow movements, reach a final towering apex; it dies away impressively into a brief, grey ending.

The stony greyness remains with the beginning of the Scherzo, which also is in D minor, and employs a fast but exact version of Ex. 13, with a new and coldly energetic theme bearing down upon it:

Ex 18 (bar 3)

This is one of Bruckner's most gigantic and fantastic scherzos: A formidable inhuman power is directly faced with heedless gaiety:

Ex 19 (bar 23)

The simple *Ländler* is introduced in F major without transition immediately after Ex 18 has driven in a quick *crescendo* to the dominant

* Published by the Bruckner Society of America.

of A, where it comes to an abrupt halt. Thematic continuity is maintained by the use in Ex. 19 of Ex. 13 (a) as a kind of *basso ostinato*, while the second violin line later becomes important in the main *Molto vivace* tempo; so perhaps the gaiety is not entirely heedless after all. But there is no denying the extraordinary gulf between the two chief characters in the drama. Here Bruckner has certainly succeeded in artistically encompassing the extremes his less critical admirers are apt to emphasize at the expense of other things.

The amiable dance measure does not last long. The key changes to D flat (*fortissimo*, bar 31), then E major (bar 39). The tempo begins to accelerate with a new figure

while Ex. 13 (a) grows forceful again. The two elements grind with magnificent harshness together and are joined by a wild figuration from the accompaniment of Ex. 19:

The drum enforces the dominant of A, but when the music reaches that key (bar 71) it is more like the dominant of D than a key in its own right. A new combination of ideas thrusts still farther forward:

It succeeds in driving home the dominant of A, and the rest of the exposition is in a breathless *pianissimo*, following the sharply arrested climax of Ex. 22 with ghostly pattering crotchets recalling the descending sevenths of the *Adagio*, ending in A at bar 131. The development begins with a return to D minor (bar 137), the drum sticking to A until bar 141, when its D plays dominant to G minor—so the tonality falls by fifths. The tension is finely held and then much increased by the sudden *fortissimo* in bar 156. C minor is screwed up to C sharp minor by a similar stroke in bar 176. Through all this, Ex. 13 assumes unpredictable shapes, and Ex. 18 is deprived of its first two bars and then inverted with the purpose (so it afterwards becomes clear) of drawing attention to a new aspect of it:

Ex. 23 (bar 172)

In C sharp minor there is a pause, and then the *Ländler* turns up again in a bland D flat (=C sharp major), performing many polyphonic tricks of the most naïve kind. When, in its third bar, the violins add Ex. 20 we can hear that this figure is that curious phenomenon a promoted derivative of Ex. 18 (b), through Ex. 23. The key changes to B major (bar 205), then minor (bar 221), then to G major (bar 225). Finally E minor (bar 233) drifts to the home dominant. Ex. 18 opens the fairly regular recapitulation in D minor, and the falling sevenths from its end dominate a short but powerful coda that ends in D major.

F sharp, the major third of D major, written as G flat, opens the Trio; it becomes a flat sixth in B flat and this marvellous little episode begins with a delicious surprise:

Ex. 24

Bruckner marks the Trio "in the same tempo", but he means that the bars, and not the crotchets, are equal to those of the Scherzo. Ex. 24 is treated with great resource and lightness of touch, as well as a delicate humour not often met in this composer. The way the first part ends in the orthodox dominant, reached by hair-raisingly unorthodox means, reveals genuine wit. The mood is felicitously and gently elated, and the one *fortissimo* passage discloses the grandeur behind it, enhancing rather than disrupting the air of easy delight. This Trio is unlike any other in Bruckner, who is normally reflective at this point in a symphony. The Scherzo returns complete.

The colossal and intricate elaboration of the Finale might seem difficult to describe, but in fact the first movement is more so. Tovey's warning that we must not expect a Bruckner finale to "go" applies with particular force to the extraordinary length of its preliminaries (which go far beyond the introductory reminiscences of previous themes that occupy the first thirty bars). When this movement does eventually "go", it is in no uncertain manner, but it would not be able to do so were it not for the protracted overtures. Once we have grasped the nature of these, we can enjoy them in much the same way as the composer must have felt them.

First comes the opening of the first movement, solemn and hushed as before, but with a soft octave figure added on a clarinet in its third and fifth bars. The quiet counterpoint this time rests on the dominant of G, and after a silence the clarinet turns the octave figure into a short phrase that seems, disconcertingly, almost comic, as the figure of poor Bruckner must have appeared to smart-alecs who had no idea what he could do:

Ex. 25 (bar 11)

Next to appear is Ex. 4, in B flat minor and turning (as it did the first time it was heard) to the dominant of D flat, where it breaks off. Ex. 25 picks up the last A flat. Now comes the theme of the *Adagio* in its original D minor. It violently conflicts with the previous suggested D flat, and Ex. 25 reminds it of the fact. We have heard enough D minor in the two previous movements, and this, not the fact that the same material begins both *Adagio* and Scherzo, is the real reason why Bruckner does not now recall the beginning of the Scherzo. To do so would be to start an argument between two unwanted keys, D minor and the dominant of D flat. Nor is Bruckner indulging in a touching imitation of Beethoven, who in the Finale of his Ninth Symphony has a philosophic purpose in drawing a harmonious theme from a background of dissonance, considering the previous movements in the light of this and finding that something utterly new is required. Bruckner recalls the old themes because it is an effective way of discussing how to get back to B flat after all that D minor. There is no question of rejecting the themes themselves, as Ex. 4 eventually becomes an important protagonist in this Finale. Now he decides that the dominant of D flat is no better than D minor; roughly, by the scruff of the neck, the cellos and basses seize Ex. 25 and turn it into a terse fugue subject in B flat:

Ex 26 (bar 31)

But this is not, as it seems at first, a real beginning. The *fugato* becomes swallowed in a march-like formal *tutti* which, instead of expanding to symphonic proportions, soon marks time on the home dominant. The totally introductory sense of everything so far is not dispelled by the amiable and cheerful new idea that now spins quietly into view in D flat:

Ex 27 (bar 67)

Indeed, this rather confirms than banishes the preludial feeling of the music, for D flat was mooted earlier. Perhaps the aggressive cellos and basses thrust B flat down the throat of D flat with too incontinent an enthusiasm? At least D flat had better be explored, to see where it may lead. (If you want to hear the connection directly, join bar 30 to bar 67, and you will find out how parenthetical the intervening passage really is.) But the only origins of D flat lie in the instability of Ex. 4, and its hold is slender as Ex. 27 runs happily and inventively about a veritable circus of keys. The figure marked (a) turns into a scale that combines with an expressive *cantabile* as E major assumes temporary control:

Ex. 28 (bar 83)

Then Ex. 27 returns in G major (bar 93). D flat, E, G—a series of minor thirds. What next—B flat? There is a *crescendo* in that direction, but if there is any key with which this section will have no truck, it is B flat. Look what it did to D flat last time! So with the deftness of a child evading a rough playmate, the music slips away into C major (bar 107). After passing through various shades and colours, including a chord (not key) of G flat (bar 121), C major shows that it was the dominant of F, for there is now a gentle full close in F major (bar 136). The innocent D flat, in avoiding B flat, has not managed to get very far away from it.

Now a big *tutti* begins in F minor, based on an augmented simplification of Ex. 25, its chromatics ironed out into plain tonic and dominant, combined with the inverted scale of Ex. 28. The bold square rhythms seem bluntly to be hewing some sort of climax, but they abruptly subside into mystery, out of which a mighty blaze of light, in the shape of a chorale on the brass, suddenly stuns the senses from the direction of a strange key:

Ex 29 (bar 175)

As the majesty of the chorale unfolds itself, its phrases interspersed with soft awed responses, the strange G flat major in which it begins proves to be but part of a wonderful and immense cadence into F major, and the music falls into a sublime calm. Horn and woodwind instruments muse over the first line of the chorale. And then? "Now," says the composer after a mere 222 bars, "we can begin!" By this time Bruckner is well out of earshot of the enemy's blasphemy, and if we wish to enter his world and taste its rewards we must also leave the enemy to grind his teeth in solitude. So now the Finale can "go".

Bruckner begins a beautiful fugue on Ex. 29; it seems to start in D flat, and at last we hear the connection between this key and B flat.

They are at once reconciled by the fact that the first phrase of the chorale turns from D flat to the dominant of B flat, and although the answer is orientated to the dominant of D flat it naturally swings round to C; the periodic combined play of the two, subject and answer, throws the music more and more surely into B flat. Soon the rhythm of Ex. 25 (there is nothing comic about it now) enters in the bass on the dominant of B flat (bar 264) and six bars later Ex. 26 makes a perfect combination with Ex. 29 in the frankest B flat minor. The two themes pass through many strange and fantastic developments, combining free inversions with themselves and each other, and the immense fugue shows astonishing resource in harmony, naïve counterpoint, instrumentation, and phrase-rhythms for 126 bars, becoming tense and mysterious at bar 306 as it enters a kind of tonal no-man's-land, growing angry, with an orchestral sound of staggering originality from bar 335 onwards. Then it hesitates momentarily. The brief break (bar 349) is enough to transform everything. There is a crash, and we discover that the music is no longer fugal but that we are being carried forward by a vigorous symphonic *tutti* that includes a grand combination of Ex. 26 and Ex. 29 and reaches a climax soon afterwards. This drastic stroke instantly solves the knotty problem of how to bring so vast a fugue to a *dénouement* within the scope of a larger symphonic whole. The *tutti* dies away with an open fifth on G flat, leading—where? To F major and the whole complex growing from Ex. 27, an unexpected and wonderfully refreshing inspiration.

This passage, its internal details often subtly changed, now has behind it a momentum it was originally without, a sense of movement irrevocably created by the fugue. On this great tide it swims where previously it paddled in the shallows; only a Bruckner could have restated the whole of an amiably indolent paragraph such as this, giving it new buoyancy and forward motion with but slight alteration. It is a matter of timing, and the effect, moreover, would not be possible without the experience of the first statement, which seemed like (and was) one of a series of static *tableaux*. A further subtlety lies in the fact that the passage, beginning in F, now ends *on* F, the dominant of B flat (see p. 144). But no—it does not end, for the new momentum means that it cannot come to a stop as it did before, and with real gaiety the music sweeps once more into a *tutti*.

This corresponds to the blunt formal *tutti* that began at bar 137, but like the previous paragraph it now has new impetus, and it is further transformed by the invasion of Ex. 4. From this moment everything grows into a vast *coda*, now contrapuntal, now massively harmonic, with myriad combinations of the themes, never losing itself in detail but always driving towards one of the greatest climaxes in symphonic music. The rule of B flat can no longer be challenged. With a mighty augmentation of Ex. 25 (bar 546) that utterly obliterates any lingering memories of the first impression made by this figure, the harmonic tension grows magnificently until it reaches a blazing chord of G flat; this proves to be the first chord of the chorale, which now strides across the whole world. The end comes with a measured precision and punctuality that mark only great composers, made possible by the fact that the chorale does not in the slightest degree slow the music down; the now stupendous momentum carries its enormous weight with ease. If Bruckner had been the kind of composer the enemy would describe, a climax of such overwhelming energy would have been impossible to him, a fact clearly unappreciated by the conductor who (proud enough of the effect to have perpetuated it on a gramophone record) halved the tempo at the entry of the chorale. Poor Bruckner —he has suffered as much from his friends as from his enemies.

We cannot leave this gigantic masterpiece without a few more observations. The first is that it is thematically more closely integrated (as the pundits say) than any of its precursors. Present-day attempts to prove the unity of large works by ingenious tissues of thematic derivations are, in my view, grossly over-valued, and stem from an obsession with Schoenbergian note rows. The actual unity of a symphonic composition is the result of interaction between all its elements. I have not shown in the foregoing analysis more than a fraction of the connections between thematic ideas in this work—the reader will find it an almost inexhaustible quarry for such research, and I would not like to spoil his pleasure in carrying it out for himself. But a warning is perhaps not out of place—believe only what you can hear! An example we have already mentioned is a reminder: Ex. 20 in the Scherzo has no connection with Ex. 18 (b) until it has been heard soon after Ex. 23. Unconscious derivations may be fascinating, but they do not necessarily have artistic significance, and no thematic manipulations (conscious or unconscious) can prove the unity, let alone the value, of a piece of music. Its real unity and its value must rest on its convincing mastery and subjugation of every single element it contains, themes, tonalities, internal rhythms, basic momentum (the upshot of all the others), as well as instrumentation, which itself can be a potent factor in the success or failure of the architecture.

Another comment that must be made concerns the internal rhythmic organization of the Fifth. The first movement needs its fairly regular arrangement of bar-periods (mostly fours) because of its basic slowness and the strangeness of its design in all other respects. The *Adagio* has many intriguing ambiguities, mainly because its overall plan is simple, and the textural intricacies (the frequent cross-rhythms) influence the larger pulses. The Scherzo is less regular than the first movement, which is natural because it has two tempi to cope with; it does not have such strange irregularities as occasionally appear in the *Adagio*, which is also natural because it has to produce an inexorable effect whenever it is fully active. The Finale is full of the most astounding irregularities, mainly arising from the fact that Ex. 26 and Ex. 29 are three-bar phrases, while the immense broadening into regularity of the coda is one of the chief elements in its impressiveness. And when the chorale stretches a vast triple rhythm over the basic quadruple pulse, the effect is overwhelming.

A large volume would not contain all that there is to be noticed in this symphony, and none of it would be trivial. Bruckner has now reached his full stature.

CHAPTER VII

SYMPHONY NO. 6, IN A MAJOR

THE FIFTH, SIXTH, and Seventh Symphonies represent Bruckner's period of greatest confidence as a composer; apart from the unfinished Ninth, they are the only ones in which he never made wholesale revisions. It is therefore doubly ironic that he never heard No. 5, and only the two middle movements of No. 6, though the Seventh was indeed to bring him luck. The A major symphony, which Bruckner thought his boldest, was not given its *première* until 1899 (three years after his death), and even then Mahler, who conducted, made great cuts in it. It is surprising that he did this, in view of his defence of the 1878 version of the much inferior Third, and in view of the fact that the Sixth is the shortest of the fully mature symphonies. It has always been neglected, and I have never been able to understand why, for it has consistently struck me (apart from one or two short passages in the Finale) as among his most beautiful and original works; his own high opinion of it seems thoroughly justified. Nor is it one of those connoisseurs' pieces—the sort of thing interesting to the thoughtful musician but not possessing immediately obvious originality. There are such works (not by Bruckner, but by others—consider, for example, Busoni's *Konzertstück* for piano and orchestra, or Alkan's Symphony for piano solo) which, though they are at a disadvantage in not revealing themselves at once as truly individual things, are nevertheless entirely so. But Bruckner's Sixth makes an instant impression of rich and individual expressiveness. Its themes are of exceptional beauty and plasticity, its harmony is both bold and subtle, its instrumentation is the most imaginative he had yet achieved, and it has, moreover, a mastery of classical form that might have impressed Brahms, especially in its first three movements. The last is more idiosyncratic, as one would expect a Bruckner finale to be, but it is profoundly original, and though there are a few uncertainties, they are minimal. It has not (nor is it intended to have) the immense impact of the last movement of No. 5, but it is a far finer and more subtle structure than that of No. 4, and its thematic material has striking individuality. We can take pleasure in agreeing with Tovey—"If we clear our minds, not only of prejudice but of wrong points of view, and treat Bruckner's Sixth Symphony

as a kind of music we have never heard before, I have no doubt that
its high quality will strike us at every moment."

The Sixth was written between 1879 and 1881; work on it over-
lapped with the revision of No. 4, finished in 1880. Its first publication
was not until after the composer was dead, in 1899, and the differences
between that edition and the manuscript seem to be entirely the responsibility of Cyril Hynais, Bruckner's pupil, who saw the symphony
through the press. They are not so extensive as might have been
inflicted by the Schalks or Loewe, but are of similar stamp, especially in
the matter of expression marks, dynamics, and tempo alterations. The
original version was published in 1935, edited by Robert Haas, and
this is the one that should always be played. The symphony opens, as
so often with Bruckner, in mystery, but with a new device, a distinctive
rhythmic figure high above a theme that heaves darkly in the depths:

Although the work is in A major and has this rhythmic beginning,
we must not expect anything like Beethoven's Seventh Symphony.
The violins' rhythm is not going to be insistent, but will be absent
for long periods, to return only at cardinal points in the structure, like
a recurring *motif* decorating cornerstones. Bruckner is careful to prevent
it from being too obtrusively lively, by indicating a bowing that keeps
on the string, and marking only the first note of each rhythmic group

staccato. It is clear that he wants it to hover over the music, not to impel it. Notice that although the key is A major when the theme enters below, the mystery is heightened by notes foreign to the tonality in the figure (c); the G is simply a flat seventh, but the B flat and F natural are Neapolitan inflexions of the melody, and they have full-scale tonal effects later in the symphony, after they have persistently coloured the harmony of the first movement. The main theme now throws off a more urgent figure:

Ex 2 (bar 15)

The last bar of Ex. 2 could easily close into F minor, but the tendency is checked by a soft settling on the home dominant at bar 21. Then a grand *fortissimo* counterstatement breaks out in the old-established classical manner. Bruckner has never done this before at the beginning of a symphony. On the great scale he has been evolving, he has not until now found out how to bring off this kind of counterstatement without impossible unwieldiness. Hitherto he has (if he ever contemplated such a device) avoided the issue either by counterstating quietly and turning in a new direction (as in the Second and Fourth), giving two statements of a whole *crescendo* process (as in the Third), or abruptly curtailing the counterstatement (as at bar 90 in the Fifth). The nearest previous approach to the classical procedure of *piano* theme and *forte* counterstatement, often found in Haydn's, Beethoven's, Dvořák's and Brahms's allegros (less often in Mozart's), is in the Fifth, but that proves to be only an incident in a tonal process already begun in the slow introduction. In the Sixth Bruckner is at last able to adjust this practice to his own time-scale, used as an actual opening, and initiating perfect sonata of huge size, and it pleases him so much that he does it again in the Seventh★ and Eighth. The counterstatement dies majestically away, again on the dominant of F (see bars 43–46); but once more this tendency is repudiated, this time by Bruckner's beloved stratagem of treating a dominant seventh as a German sixth in a new key, a delight he shares with Schubert. So instead of F we get E minor, and a broad theme in rather slower tempo:

★ As we shall see, its function in No. 7 is not sonata-like.

Ex 3 (bar 49)

The mood is nobly contemplative, grave but not static. The texture is exquisitely beautiful and the whole passage is notable for the complexity of its inner (as opposed to the grand simplicity of its outer) rhythms. Other tonalities colour the music, the dominant of G flat at bar 61 *et seq.*, and an angelic new theme on the wind is finely illumined by touches of D major and F major:

Ex 4 (bar 69)

Throughout this paragraph the music is marvellously embroidered with intricate patterns of sixths and sevenths (very different from the sevenths so forthrightly used in the Fifth and even more different from Elgar's), and Neapolitan inflexions abound in delicate forms. The passing gleams of foreign keys do not really disturb E, and at bar 81 Ex. 3 swells out radiantly in E major. It fades, and a slow *crescendo* begins to rise on the dominant of E (bar 95). This reaches a massive new theme, not in E, but on its flat sixth, C, another Neapolitan relationship:

Ex 5 (bar 101)

Inevitably the C falls to B, the dominant of E (bar 107), then comes back again at the next *piano* with a new idea (woodwind, bar 111). The triplet in Ex. 5 becomes pervasive and the music swings over alien dominants to that of G major (bar 121); note this, for it is the source of a fine and simple stroke in the recapitulation. Then G leads to C (bar 129), A minor (bar 131) and a spacious and peaceful plagal cadence in E major. During this process the idea that was new at bar 111 has undergone cunning transformations which I leave the reader to examine at his leisure. We are now at the end of the exposition. The extent and the nature of this wonderfully calm and elaborate second group has shown the unwisdom of expecting propulsive energy from the rhythm of Ex. 1 (a)—it was, after all, a mode of vibration.

Nor must we expect an immediate return to anything like strenuous action. The development at first stays ruminating about the environs of E major, then its supertonic, F sharp minor, twists unexpectedly into G major with a new treatment in free inversions of Ex. 1 (b) and (c) (bar 159). The music's muscles are beginning slowly to flex again, though the rhythm of Ex. 1 (a) is still not in evidence. With lazy but large stride it swings into A minor (bar 167), C major (bar 175), and then, with a definite sense of effort, to the dominant of D flat (bar 181). In D flat come derivatives of Ex. 2; the growth in dynamics and the rising tonalities have made tension, and the livelier rhythm of Ex. 2 now gathers itself together. All the while a continuous quaver triplet motion has been sustained. With this, Ex. 2 now drives into a powerful *crescendo* on a dissonance that soon proves itself the dominant of E flat. In E flat Ex. 1, now accompanied by the throb of (a), crashes out *ff*. The *tutti* moves magisterially through G flat and A flat and then, astoundingly, straight into A major for the recapitulation. No wonder Bruckner thought this his boldest symphony—we shall find that one of its chief characteristics is this startling ability to establish (without a shadow of doubt as to its solidity) the tonic with hairbreadth abruptness, and with the kind of preparation that would normally be expected to undermine it. This A major is the opposite pole from the E flat from which the *tutti* started. It is immediately prepared by but two bars of its own dominant seventh (bars 207–8), a chord, moreover, were it not for the low E on the drum, we might expect to behave like a German sixth in the previous key of A flat. But it is the drum that does the trick. Bruckner is often conservatively classical in his use of the timpani, and has learned much from Beethoven, who sometimes achieves great subtleties by relying on the fact that the drum is not a transposing instrument, and that its notes, if (as hitherto) they are restricted to two (tonic and dominant), cannot possibly be genuinely enharmonic. Basil Lam, in the chapter on Beethoven in *The Symphony*,* has pertinently observed how that master in the first movement of his Fourth Symphony makes the drum enter with a low B flat near the end of the development, when the music is on the dominant of B natural major; on any other instrument we would interpret this B flat as A sharp, but the associations of that note with the drum's natural behaviour make the tonic B flat thenceforward inescapable, and the magnificent solidity of the recapitulation is assured.

And so it is at the recapitulation in Bruckner's Sixth. As soon as the drum enters on its low E we know, without a trace of uncertainty and whatever the notation might look like (in this case, as it happens, it is written as a normal dominant seventh in A), that this note is not F flat, but E. Bruckner's stroke is amazingly abrupt, especially considered in relation to the time-scale of the movement as a whole. It and those of Beethoven stand alone—at any rate, it is difficult to think of another example anywhere else in symphonic music. If Bruckner's idea were inspired by Beethoven, is it not revealing that it should be the naïve Bruckner who saw the point? Or should we perhaps revise our ideas about Bruckner's naïvety? I think the latter, and if Bruckner thought of it without reference to Beethoven, even more should we be careful about underestimating him. One often meets aesthetes who point to the superiority, the greater "purity", of the string quartet medium as opposed to the orchestral; but every medium has its unique possibilities, and this particular profound subtlety would be impossible in a string quartet. There is a lot to be said, too, for the classical restriction of the timpani to two or three basic notes if it stimulates a composer to such thought. That this is one of the greatest moments in Bruckner's music I have no doubt.

Statement and counterstatement are now reversed, the soft one coming afterwards at bar 229. It turns to the dominant of F sharp; there is now no manœuvring with German sixths, ambiguous or otherwise,

---

* Pelican, 1967, edited by the present writer.

and the second group follows with Ex. 3 in F sharp minor. Why not the tonic minor? We shall see. Except for changes in the orchestration, a slight curtailment after Ex. 4 that brings in the radiant major version of Ex. 3 a few bars sooner, and a poetic alteration before the entry of Ex. 5, the second group is restated exactly, with the same tonal and harmonic relationships as before. We then find that the G major 6/4 harmony of bars 121–4 has become A major in bars 305–8. If Bruckner has recapitulated the second group in A minor he would now be in C, and would have to spend as long getting back to A as he did recovering E major at the end of the exposition. After so dramatic a start to the whole recapitulation, he needs a more or less regular restatement of the second group, but he needs also to save space before what is going to be one of his broadest and finest codas. Hence the submediant recapitulation of the second group, in a quiet environ of the tonic major, which now can be reached as unassumingly as it was shatteringly recaptured earlier. So as soon as the sound of A major is heard at bar 305, it is as familiar as the view from one's own window.

Tovey rightly describes the *coda* of this movement as one of Bruckner's greatest passages. I am not sure, however, that he is quite to the point in remarking that Wagner might have been content to sign it. There is nothing Wagnerian about the music, and certainly not about the masterly abruptness of the return to the tonic at the end, which is entirely typical of this symphony, and which might have caused Wagner a few qualms. But Wagner would have fully appreciated the wonderful iridescent colours of this part of the movement, perfectly described by Tovey—"passing from key to key beneath a tumultuous surface sparkling like the Homeric seas". The main theme rises and falls like some great ship, the water illuminated in superb hues as the sun rises, at last bursting clear in the sky. During this coda Bruckner passes through the entire spectrum of tonality; there is no key that he does not suggest in its sixty bars, but A is the only fixed point and it is salutary to contemplate the unerring accuracy of his draughtsmanship as he hovers round subdominant, tonic, dominant, and submediant in bars 327–36, precisely half-way between the beginning of the coda and its final mighty plagal cadence, in which the drum makes a tremendous effect by playing a D for the first time. A further contributory factor to the impression of enormous strength is the fact that in this *coda* every single basic harmony, except for the two bars penultimate to the final tonic, is a triad in root position.

In the *Adagio*, too, we find Bruckner at his deepest. The frequent

E

Neapolitan inflexions of the first movement, beginning with the B flat and F in the main theme itself, make it natural that the *Adagio* should be in F, with an opening, moreover, that seems to be at first in B flat minor. Like most of Bruckner's largest designs, the first movement has a huge range of modulation, but it is worth noting that the key of F is rarely more than hinted in it, and never once established. Yet the first cardinal move was in that very direction, when the dominant seventh of F was turned into a German sixth in E minor just before the second group began. So the sound of the *Adagio* is both related to and contrasted with that of the first movement. Here we explore a world on which windows have but briefly been opened, but which we have known was always there. In such ways it is that each successive movement of a mature Bruckner symphony is like a layer uncovered.

This movement is one of the largest and most perfectly realized slow sonata designs since the *Adagio sostenuto* of Beethoven's *Hammerklavier* sonata. It is often played too fast; it will both withstand and reward the slowest playing that artistry, technique, and courage can afford. The feeling is elegiac, and the first great phrase of the main theme begins in the shadows of B flat minor, moving towards the light and the dominant of F major:

It is joined by haunting oboe phrases:

The first phrase is of four bars; then, when Ex. 7 begins, two two-bar units move into two of one bar each. This creates tension without destroying the magistral growth of the line, and the music broadens again to a climax at bar 13, with F major now affirmed. The violins take up the dejected rhythm of Ex. 7 as it falls away from the climax; then solemn descending motives derived from Ex. 6 (b) sink into darkness. The whole vast melody (for such it is) seems about to close in F,

when the horns make a deliberate modulation in the unforeseen
direction of E major (this is not Bruckner's favourite transformation of
the dominant seventh into a German sixth, as it might very well have
been, but a much more solid modulation that prepares the ear for E
as a new tonic; yet it is less conclusive that it would have been with
dominant preparation, for he uses instead diminished harmony over
a subdominant pedal—originally the third in the key of F—thus making
a very beautiful and pathetic plagal cadence). The sense of sorrow is
greatly softened by the lovely new counterpoint of themes that now
sings in E major:

Ex 8 (bar 25)
(principal parts only)

This exquisite music does not stay in E major. It burgeons in a C
major climax and, instead of slipping back to the dominant of E (as
such apparently Neapolitan harmony normally would), C major
remains floating in the air. It is the orthodox and most natural key for
the second group of an F major sonata movement, but it is approached
in the finest imaginable way; at the same time we have yet another
distinguished example of the Schubertian-Brucknerian second group
that contains its own transition. The light of C major fades slowly,
and in time there comes another new theme, a grieving funeral march
in C minor, with an expressive A flat major tinge:

Ex 9 (bar 53)

It drifts away from C minor, and at bar 69 the immensely broad
development begins with Ex. 6 (a) in A flat minor, its descending bass
now above it in the woodwind. In inexorable stages it climbs until it
reaches the home dominant with the natural melodic sequel, Ex. 6 (b)
(bar 75). But though the recapitulation is already suggested, the oboe
(which has a marvellous part to play in this movement) turns the music

into B flat. Here the inversion of Ex. 6 (a) is in the bass, in free canon with bassoons and clarinets, and with an aspiring new line on the violins. Feeling rises as the harmony clouds, and with remarkable simplicity and economy a climax of some intensity is generated, no key being fixed, with the inversion of Ex. 6 (b) in the bass. It leaves the tail of Ex. 6 (b) (inverted) floating in space with wisps of *appoggiature* in clarinet and oboe above it, and the air is desolate as the oboe is left alone (bar 92).

Now the recapitulation begins, with characteristic movement in the violins as the great theme returns on the horns. The descending bass pulsates darkly, and it is very touching to hear the way the last lone cry of the oboe proves to have been an anticipation of Ex. 7. The whole complex of Ex. 6–7 is now caught up in a *crescendo-diminuendo* paragraph of the highest tragic grandeur whose threnody seems almost irrevocable—until the pall of F minor vanishes; Ex. 8 in F major, sweeps all the grief away. It will be remembered that when this theme first came in E major, the modulation was unexpected, and the E major itself proved part of a transition to C major, then minor with Ex. 9. This time it is in the tonic, and its inevitability is such that the whole great troubled paragraph before it seems to have been only its preparation. There is now no question of the second group having its own internal transition; this is unequivocally the home key. Yet the same climax occurs, now in C sharp major (which is to F what C was to E in the exposition), but its sequel is now Ex. 9 in the tonic F minor instead of C sharp minor, and this retrospectively gives it new meaning. The whole restatement of the second group is thus given a fresh function, and it would be cruel to make the cut suggested in the first publication—from the end of the first-group paragraph (bar 112) to the return of Ex. 9 (bar 133). Tovey says, "Reluctantly, perhaps on Bruckner's part, certainly on mine, the orthodox recapitulation . . . is shortened at the composer's suggestion". It was Hynais's suggestion, not Bruckner's; the composer could scarcely have been more reluctant to accept it, for he was dead at the time.

The fine-drawn consolatory coda is one of Bruckner's best. Ex. 9 having moved away from F minor on to the dominant of D flat, the little semiquaver figure from Ex. 8 restores the home dominant, rises to an impassioned moment in A flat (bar 145), and eventually eases into the main theme, at last in a serene F major. This ultimate stage is among Bruckner's wisest and tenderest utterances. Although it is entirely his own natural voice, it is moving evidence that he has taken

Die Meistersinger to heart. The sanity and kindliness of the music is
Hans Sachs's as well as Bruckner's.

The Scherzo is quite unlike any other by this composer, slower than
usual, often shadowed and muted, but sometimes brilliant with flashes
in the dark. It is in A minor. Frequently it has been said to anticipate
Mahler, especially perhaps the middle movement (marked *Schattenhaft*)
of his Seventh Symphony; I am inclined to think that while Mahler
may well have been influenced by Bruckner's piece (he did, after all,
conduct it) there is really little in common between the two. Mahler
may certainly look back at and be stimulated by certain aspects of
Bruckner, but there is nothing in this Scherzo that looks forward to
the nightmarish quality of Mahler's inspirations. It is mysterious, but
rooted in calm. Its steady 3/4 time is mostly pervaded by triplets, and
one gets the impression rather of 9/8; the basic triple time builds itself
into extremely broad four-bar pulses, so that the actual sense of movement is remarkably deliberate for a scherzo. Bruckner marks it *Nicht
schnell* and indeed it is really an *allegretto*. Quiet though much of it is,
and delicate, it nevertheless creates a sense of suppressed power. We
are out in the night with owls and blown leaves, and the sharp tiny
glint of unthinkably alien stars. We sense a soft drumming in the earth.
A door flies wide with a flare of light and din; there is the smith and
the anvil. At all events, there is no nightmare in this music—only
wonder.

The deep simplicity of the structure is worth reflecting upon. In the
whole of the first part of the Scherzo there are but two bass notes, E
and A, and the first twenty large bars are on a dominant pedal. When
the bass moves at last to A it is not the tonic, but the bottom of a
6/3 chord of F major (bar 21). The bass sticks to A through diminished harmony (bar 33) and then drops back to E when the first section
ends in E major at bar 43. So there has not yet been a single root chord
of A minor. Ex. 10 shows the main theme over its dominant pedal.

The subdued development stays around D flat, G flat, and B flat
minor, all closely related to each other, but mysteriously remote from
the tonic. Then, with a stirring of ambiguous diminished harmony,
the home dominant is reached at bar 75. The recapitulation begins, as
before, over a dominant pedal. Still no root chord of A minor! There
are alterations in detail, and now the music passes through the dominant
of D flat (bar 89) before the blacksmith hammers on the dominant of A,
bending it powerfully into A major. So the recapitulation, compared
with the exposition, is extravagant in the matter of bass notes; it has no

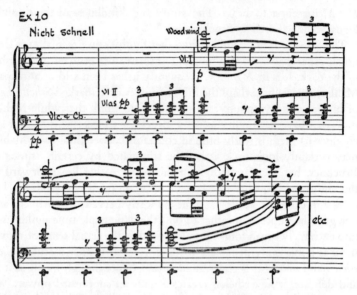

less than three, E, A flat, and A natural, and this last is the first root
chord of the tonic in the whole piece.

The Trio is something utterly indescribable; Tovey again, perhaps—
"Strange *pizzicato* chords and rhythms introduce the three horns of
Beethoven's Eroica Symphony into the *Urwald* of Wagner. The violins
pronounce a solemn blessing in their cadences." To this I would add
that Beethoven and Wagner are also introduced to the main theme of
Bruckner's Fifth Symphony, and express their astonishment when
shown what it is like upside down. The impassioned magic of this short
C major movement is not like anything else. We can analyse it as
meticulously as we like, but will not be able to explain why in every
detail the unexpected is inevitable, and the inevitable totally unexpected. One of Bruckner's favourite harmonic gambits has something to do with it; the opening *pizzicati* seem to be on the dominant
of D flat, but the horns imperiously insist that this must of course be a
German sixth in C major:

Whereupon the woodwind opt for a compromise with the theme of the Fifth in A flat, but the horns turn stubbornly back towards C and gain the acquiescence (or solemn blessing) of the strings—that is, until they immediately remember the *pizzicati* on the dominant of D flat. So we go through the same motions again, to end the first part. The second part seems to favour the direction of A flat and D flat, but as a *crescendo* rises there is intense feeling that C major should after all be the right key. It stimulates a poetic debate that finally brings the committee back to the original exchange between *pizzicati* and horns. This time the woodwind give their inimitable rendering of the theme of the Fifth upside down—but they still like A flat. It slightly shakes the opinion of horns and strings, but the latter find that C major is really all right. Everyone is compelled to agree that this is proper preparation for the return of the Scherzo.

In the chapter on the Fourth Symphony I tried to give some idea of the kind of finale Bruckner was instinctively aiming at (see p. 94). We saw in the ensuing analysis how in that symphony the solution to the problem was obscured by irrelevant sonata habits. In the Fifth he triumphantly mastered a new kind of finale, aided by the vast fugal development of much of the music and the generative power of thematic combination. All this created in that mighty structure a momentum of a sort unprecedented in symphonic music. But it is not quite the type of momentum aimed at unsuccessfully in the finale No. 3 and No. 4 and totally achieved in that of No. 8. The last movement of the Sixth shows a stage intermediate between these, but it is far nearer to the success of the Eighth than it is to the hesitancy of the earlier works. No. 6 does not demand so colossal a finale as No. 8, for its general dimensions are smaller, but it is here that Bruckner, with an occasional moment of puzzlement, first manages to reveal the new essence with real mastery. The distillation of an essence must result in something plainer than the brew from which it is distilled, and since, as we have seen, this kind of Bruckner finale expresses the nature from which the rest of the symphony has arisen, we must expect it to concentrate more directly (or, better, more obviously) on vast slow motion, with a corresponding reduction in elaboration of texture. On the other hand, as we shall see, the tonal conflicts that underlie the invention in the rest of the symphony are now to be laid bare—so in this sense the finale is going to reveal a more complex situation; but for this very reason its textures must be simpler. Nothing essential must be concealed beneath a decorative surface; nor must the true nature of the progression be hidden or smoothed over by well lubricated transitions. Empty space must be part of the composition and it, too, must be so ordered that the great momentum passes steadily through it. The placing of block against block and mass against void must of itself create its own comprehensively deliberate rhythm. The listener has to feel Bruckner's sense of time, and there lies a snare for many; we all have different built-in animal clocks, and some have more patience than others. But it is possible to adjust such an internal clock—in fact we are all doing it all the time, and can easily do so whenever we need or really want to. Once we have found the correct adjustment, we are able to hear the tick of Bruckner's and even to notice when it falters; we shall surely know when synchronization is achieved. Being then literally sympathetic, we are entitled to criticize.

The Finale of the Sixth (*which must not be played too fast*) begins on the dominant of A minor with a severe theme that stresses the flat sixth (F):

Ex 12 Bewegt doch nicht zu schnell

Nocturnal mystery pervades the air as Ex. 12 moves to the dominant of D minor (bar 19), its flat sixth now being B flat. These two "Neapolitan" notes (F and B flat) were also prominent in the main theme of the first movement, and the tonalities of F and B flat were basic to the *Adagio*. They will be found to make deep and disturbing inroads on the Finale. At the end of bar 22 horns and trumpets peremptorily inject the sound of A major into the music, with startling effect, and their interruptions engender a massively marching *tutti* in the tonic major:

Ex 13 (bar 29)

At bar 37 the brass deliver another powerful theme, consisting mainly of F and B flat:

B flat minor briefly becomes the tonality; then, with the aid of Ex. 13 (b) Bruckner lifts everything back on to the home dominant, where Ex. 14 (a) dominates another *tutti* (bar 53). The stiff-necked insistence with which it closes by hammering the dominant chord is caused by the force with which A major was invaded by the B flat minor of Ex. 14, and the conductor who does not realize this will speed up here. A horn is left holding an E that is still the dominant of A. But instead of the tonic comes a typical Bruckner *Gesangsperiode* beginning in C major (exactly the same relationship can be found in the Finale of No. 5, letter B):

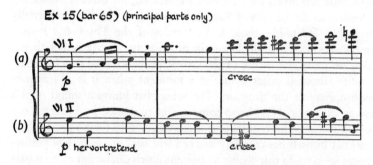

This C major is neutral—it could be either the relative major of A minor or the dominant of F. The childlike innocence recalls the corresponding passage in the Finale of the Second Symphony, and this is equally beautiful, though more easily disturbed. Like all such episodes in Bruckner it moves in guileless two- and four-bar phrases and soon begins to roam harmonically. It becomes a little introspective and by bar 88 seriously considers the possibility of B flat. But this is brightly contradicted by—of course—A major, in the next bar. This turns to the minor and by a devious and exquisitely expressive route returns the music to C major at bar 97. This time the tendency to introspection causes clouded harmony (bar 105), and Ex. 15 (b) gets caught in an irresistible *crescendo* on the dominant of F. But the situation is saved by the majestic entry of Ex. 14, augmented and inverted, on the dominant of E (bar 125). It lets drop a new derivative—

Ex 16 (bar 130)

before resuming its striving to assert E. Abruptly its efforts are cut off, and a low F is heard pulsing quietly in the bass (bar 145). Over this, Ex. 16 asks anxious questions, and with growing agitation searches blindly for key after key. It drags the bass and the harmony with it, bar by bar. At bar 156 it actually hits on E major but staggers on, still confused. At last it finds the dominant of E (bar 163) and holds pathetically on to E major until bar 175.

But E major cannot now be convincingly established; the last quiet shock of F at bar 145 was too much for it. We must confess that it was also a little too much for Bruckner's invention, for there is something pedestrian in the labours of Ex. 16; but a fault of this kind is partially forgivable, for unlike those in the finales of the Third and Fourth symphonies, it is a slight lowering of inventive power rather than a failure to grasp the nature of the artistic problem. And it is fortunate that the laboured effect comes at a moment when it is at least not inappropriate to the situation. The somewhat lumpish sound of this passage can, moreover, be to some extent mitigated by bringing out the rich sustained harmonies of trombones and tuba (bars 151–8) which Bruckner himself has carefully marked *sehr stark und breit*; few performances seem to do this properly. But not much can be done about bars 167–74, and speeding them up impatiently is no answer.

E major, uncertainly seated, begins to sound like a dominant, and with a natural reduction of the tempo Ex. 12 again hovers gloomily in its original tonal position (bar 177). Ex. 16 asks more questions, at first still on the dominant of A minor, then moving tentatively towards either D minor or F major. Inevitably the uncertainty is for the time being resolved in favour of F major, and philosophically accepting the fact, the inversion of Ex. 12 sings calmly in the cellos with broad serene harmonization, creating an atmosphere curiously anticipatory of Sibelius's Sixth Symphony. More warmth comes with a turn to A flat (bar 203), C major (bar 207), and E flat major (bar 209).

Movement gathers when the second violins play Ex. 12 (no longer inverted) on the dominant of A flat minor (bar 211), but so does a sense of foreboding. The brass answer powerfully with Ex. 13 (b) on the same dominant. Softly and persistently the treatment of Ex. 12 continues, rising in pitch and volume. The brass (bar 225) hit the dominant of A with Ex. 13 (b), but increase the tension by immediately blazing out the same motive a semitone higher, on the dominant of B flat. The tonal argument is still being hotly pursued. A horn takes up Ex. 14 which can now, after the preceding developments, clearly be heard as an inverted derivative of Ex. 12; it rises with it to the dominant of E flat (bar 234). The heavy brass answer with the second half of the theme, and screw up the tension still further by authoritatively compelling it upwards, step by step, to the dominant of B flat. The music has already staved off an invasion from the direction of F, at first by severe effort, then by philosophic persuasion. What is the answer now to an obviously formidable challenge from the other terrible twin, B flat?

The reply at first hesitates on the dominant of D flat, but then the full orchestra defiantly crashes into a clear A major with Ex. 13. The effect of this is so overwhelming that a magnificently spacious *tutti* is able to march unimpeded for forty bars. It is not, however, entirely undisturbed, for A major's shock tactics in the face of B flat cannot establish it beyond doubt. Soon it turns to D minor (bar 253), which turns dominant minor to G minor, and then moves down through the dominant of F minor to A flat (bar 261). At bar 265 there is a sudden *piano* on the dominant of A, then as a *crescendo* grows, A minor takes over (bar 269). The key of A is being consolidated. A minor shifts to C major (bar 277), then D minor (bar 279), and then G flat major, which is really F sharp (bar 281). The music has now climbed over the top of A, and can easily descend to its dominant, which it does at bar 285. All this listing of keys and modulations naturally makes appallingly dull reading and gives no idea of the wonderful majesty of the music. (I can see the reviewer fiercely writing, "To take your points in order, yes it does and no it doesn't!", but we must not forget that he should have no cause for complaint; he is no ordinary reader and should understand these things, not be bored by them. Let us waste no pity on him, though it is regrettable that musical jargon is so deadeningly unmusical and that there is no other way of describing how the music works—a necessary task in the case of so frequently misunderstood a composer as Bruckner.)

Fragments of the *tutti* fall slowly over what is now clearly the home dominant, and come to rest. Then, in A major, Ex. 15 begins to sing once more. Originally it appeared in a neutral, non-committal key; now it gladly confirms the tonic. But it wanders as it did before and eventually arrives at B flat, where it hesitates doubtfully (bar 330). All is not well yet. A chord of C flat is suggested; the horns hold it, waiting. C flat is B, the dominant of E—perhaps this looks hopeful? So the plaintive and rather hapless Ex. 16 timidly tries this possibility. It gathers confidence, but the more it does, the further astray goes its aim. This figure is like Bruckner in Viennese society, it blunders about. At bar 356 it stops dead, nonplussed in E flat minor. It starts again, slowly (oboe and clarinet), and is actually staring uncomprehendingly at the dominant of A. Once more it turns in the wrong direction, this time becoming excited—but it is the dominant of F. The *crescendo* is cut off (bar 370) on the edge of a precipice; B flat minor is creeping malevolently at the bottom of it (letter X). Ex. 13 again comes to the rescue with a militant blaze of A major (letter Y), but the terrible fascination of B flat minor is too much—again we stare over the fearsome cliff at the thing below (bar 397). But no!—resolutely Bruckner turns his back on it, and the A major sun is high in the sky as he strides towards it (letter Z). At the end the theme of the first movement lends its voice to the reassurance.

So ends this fantastic, almost surrealistic movement, leaving dark questions unanswered. Despite the small flaws connected with Ex. 16, it is a masterpiece of astounding originality, and if we want to have some idea of the range that exists within Bruckner's consciousness, we need only compare what this Finale expresses with what is to be found in its predecessor in the Fifth Symphony. Even the faults here have some point, for the *gaucherie* with which Ex. 16 is handled is in a sense functional. This figure, incidentally, bears at times a close resemblance to Ex. 7 in the *Adagio*, as if that pathetic motive, dignified in its own surroundings, now is bewildered in an alien world. Is this too fanciful an idea, or could Bruckner have meant that? So far as the structure of this Finale is concerned, it is only too obvious that its various stages can be interpreted by rule of thumb as those of a sonata movement: second group, bar 65, development, bar 177, recapitulation, bar 245, *coda*, some time after letter V—all very comfortingly easy, provided we are willing to forget conveniently where the real tensions of the piece are distributed. They are in the extraordinary triangular conflict between A on the one hand and F and B flat on the other, and in exploring the depths of so-called Neapolitan relationships Bruckner instinctively arrives at an unprecedented form, in which elements of thematic treatment and recapitulation are as inevitable as they are in most music extended beyond aphoristic limits. Bruckner's instinct has now broken through the barriers of his own prejudices, and it is not surprising if he himself thought the Sixth his most daring work. Of all his completed symphonies it is the least conclusive, in the easy sense of the word; yet in it he comes to far-reaching conclusions about his own artistic constitution, and embodies them in a profound work of art.

CHAPTER VIII

SYMPHONY No. 7, IN E MAJOR

IT IS SOMETIMES suggested that the Sixth Symphony, with its richness of harmony and line and the refinement of its orchestration, is more interesting as an anticipation of the Seventh (completed in 1883) than it is in itself. Such a view is nonsensical, and is typical of the superficiality of much Bruckner criticism. It is true that No. 6 is in many ways a new departure, in the respects just mentioned; but whereas it is, especially in its first three movements, a climax in Bruckner's mastery of his own kind of sonata music, only one movement of No. 7 (the Scherzo) is in true sonata form. The other three movements are evolved along entirely individual lines, with a special functioning of tonality and a spacing of calm and climax that is apt to peculiar purposes. On paper the first movement of the Seventh looks like a clumsily formed sonata design with its tensions in the wrong places, and was, indeed, once used by H. C. Colles in this very way to demonstrate what a good composer was Brahms by comparison with the inept Bruckner. Such semblances may easily fool the routined critic; a proper analysis of such music as this must be conducted (*a*) with a completely accurate ear for tonalities and the ability to relate (not merely rationalize) tonal experiences over large stretches, and (*b*) with freedom from conventional *a priori* concepts. The work must be followed from point to point with the aid of a retentive memory for details intelligently observed and understood, and without reliance on impossible diagrams or misleading ground-plans. The hoary legend that would have Bruckner an inspired yokel still dies hard, and is a comforting substitute for hard thought and careful observance. I hope that in this book the legend is already showing signs of wear, and if we want finally to see through it, the Seventh Symphony (which is one of Bruckner's greatest and most original works) should give us the opportunity. And there need be no fear that thinking clearly and thoroughly about it will weaken the magic of its indestructible beauty; this is the most obviously beautiful of all the symphonies, and its artistry is of the kind that can only gain power from scrutiny.

That the Seventh is so widely loved is evidence that the impression it makes is direct. Its flowing melody and the intensity of its harmony are finely matched, and the sound of its orchestra gives off a golden gleam. In expression it ranges from exalted serenity to funereal sorrow, and its last two movements are the most purely joyous Bruckner wrote. Nobility speaks from every measure of it. We are about to examine it, but let no one imagine that the subtleties we shall uncover have nothing to do with the satisfying qualities the sympathetic but lay listener finds in hearing the symphony. They have everything to do with them. The vast mental, neural, and muscular complexities that underlie a smile have not yet been analysed; but everyone understands a smile, and without these complexities (which are decidedly not mechanics in the crude sense of the term) no smile could exist. Bruckner's music, fortunately, does not have that kind of complexity (at least so far as concerns the kind of analysis we are capable of); we can perhaps hope to get from it the sort of satisfaction that might come from scrutinizing, rather than merely reacting to, a smile. No analysis can make great music out of poor, or dredge up subtleties without testing them against their effects. The ordinary listener need not be afraid; we shall not get lost in subtleties—their effects are too powerful, even on the majority who have no interest in trying to find out why. But the misunderstandings of decades have piled into a debt we must attempt to repay. So to perdition with further apologies; let us look at the score with our ears.

The entrance to No. 7 (Bruckner's favourite string *tremolo*) leads to a very lofty and light interior:

Ex 1 (bar 3)

Notice how this magnificent arching theme modulates to the dominant before slipping back to the tonic for a fully scored counterstatement. It is of the highest importance. The rich counterstatement (beginning at letter A, bar 25)* shows the same tendency, but it is checked by a beautiful cloudy elongation that finally settles *on* (not *in*) the dominant. The distinction between being "in" or "on" the dominant is a very real one, not always fully grasped by writers on music. At the end of the first statement of the theme, in bar 23, we are about to settle *in* the key of B major, for Bruckner has modulated from the original E major so decisively that the new key is about to take possession as of right. Bar 24 shows how he has to get back to the first tonic at the last moment, rather drastically. In other words, he has made B major momentarily a new tonic. We are in it, and until the 24th bar are expecting it to remain. Since B is the dominant of E, we speak of being in the dominant. If we are *on* the dominant, it is functioning only as a chord, not as a key, and feels as if it wants to fall back to the tonic. At letter B in the score (bar 51) the note B does not feel like a tonic; if the music were to stop there it would not sound like a close—we would expect a chord of E major at the beginning of the next bar to create a sense of rest. To be *in* the dominant is to be in a key: to be *on* it is simply to have the sensation of a chord, or penultimate harmony. To some readers this will seem elementary; there are, however, respected books on classical music which show no awareness of the distinction, committing frequent howlers.

What we are about to witness is a long process that is adumbrated by this tendency of the main theme to modulate into B major. Throughout the whole first part of the movement B major takes over, as it were, by stealth, in a manner remote from the muscular action of sonata. At bar 51 the chord of B major is still a dominant, but with quiet deliberation oboe and clarinet, supported by soft horns and trumpet, bring in a new theme, and treat B as if it were a key:

Ex 2 (bar 51)

---

* Bar numbers and rehearsal letters refer to the Bruckner Society score edited by Robert Haas.

As the quotation shows, B major becomes B minor (bar 52) and in
bar 53 loses its slender foothold. For the next 18 bars the music drifts
through a series of remoter harmonies, but returns to a chord of B
major at bar 69. The chord is a 6/4 (i.e. with F sharp in the bass); it
strengthens without establishing the influence of B. The flow grows in
confidence and the tonality is carried to the crest of a wave, then falls
into C major harmony, definitely felt as the flat supertonic of B
(bar 77, letter C). The phrase of Ex. 2 now has a new ending which
becomes absorbed in a short but lovely triple counterpoint:

Ex 3 (bar 81)(principal parts only)

The Neapolitan C major falls easily back into B major (bar 89),
which now shows a confidence that is not undermined by the "passing
keys", through which it moves almost at once. These occupy 10 bars,
and at bar 103 the iron grip of a deep pedal F sharp settles the firm
entrenchment of B, toward which tonality a giant *crescendo* sweeps.
Throughout this process Ex. 2 has prevailed. The first big climax comes
with a sudden hush and a rhythmic new theme in B minor:

Ex 4 (bar 123)

Passing through harmonies of F sharp minor, D major and minor, and G flat major (= F sharp major), this rises quickly to a massive brass fanfare, afterwards closing gently in B major. Ex. 4 and its sequel should not be regarded only as a "third subject". Analysis often pays attention to the themes without due regard to their function; the sudden change of character at this moment is caused by the release of tension arising from the victory of B, and it provides, as well as a new theme, a welcome change of movement. We shall find that when Ex. 4 is recapitulated much further on in the movement, it serves an entirely different purpose.

Outward resemblances such as the change from tonic (E) to dominant (B) must not deafen us to the fact that such behaviour as we find in this opening section is totally uncharacteristic of sonata. The slow emergence of one key, by persuasion, from a region dominated by another is a new phenomenon in the field of symphony, and the rest of this movement will be heard to reinstate E major in a similar but longer process. We shall find that E major, in fact, is not fully restored until the end of the movement. During this process, material is bound to be recapitulated; such restatement is far from conventional, helpless, or redundant, as we shall see. Recapitulation is, after all, a prime element in any large-scale form, whether its motion is sonata-like or not. The assertion that Bruckner was haplessly fettered to useless sonata formulae breaks down when it is understood that elements a lesser master might have made into a clumsy development, restatement, and coda are here welded into a single organic structure, the natural consequent of the opening section. This movement is composed against the background of sonata, but it is something new.

Two horns augment the closing notes of the last group (bar 163) and a clarinet peacefully plays an inversion of Ex. 1 (a) in B major. An oboe freely imitates it, gently supported by trombones. After a flute echo of figures from the Ex. 4 paragraph, the mode becomes minor with another entry of the clarinet-oboe-trombones combination. This time the flute hints at the dominant of A flat, but a solemn inversion of Ex. 2 follows in D minor on cellos. It breaks off, and is heard again high in the violins in E minor, at present not recognizable as the tonic minor. The cellos take it up again in F sharp minor, whence it grows into a grandly sustained *cantabile* with a trend towards E minor. F sharp is soon shown to have been a supertonic harmony. Very definite emphasis is laid on E minor by the abrupt but quiet interruption of Ex. 4 in that key, on a solo flute (the basses playing a mirror inversion) (bar 219). Violins join with a new counterpoint. E minor is then contradicted quickly by A minor, D major, D minor, C major, B flat major, and A flat major. A drop to *ppp* finds the music waiting expectantly on the dominant of C, then a beat's silence is shattered by a powerful outburst in C minor. The inversion of Ex. 1 (a) strides grimly across the orchestra in an imitative passage that lasts for 16 bars. When the irruption subsides, C minor is in firm control.

Here is a crucial incident that shows plainly the gulf between sonata principles and those obeyed by Bruckner in this movement. He is now approaching the moment usually construed as a sonata restatement. Consider first the effect of this massive C minor passage, like a great dam placed across a river. This dam does not create a swamp or even a lake, for music is not water, but it postpones for a time a return of the normal flow, and (in purely musical terms which we had better hastily restore) it puts off indefinitely the establishment of the home key. In a sonata movement on this scale such a passage would inevitably generate the kind of tension demanding a long preparation for the recapitulation, which would come with the effect of a well planned uprising, even if it were quiet. This does not happen here.

The music calms but there is no immediate change of key. The first theme begins in C minor with euphonious echoes in the woodwind and a gracious counterpoint in the first violins, and then it modulates to the dominant of D (bar 257). In D minor the same thought recurs, now turning in the direction of A flat. There is a *crescendo*—but the expected A flat is magically supplanted by E major. The whole of Ex. 1 is now stated for the first time since the outset (bar 281). E major is just appreciable as the tonic because of Bruckner's strategic handling of E minor before the big C minor passage (see bar 219). But its position is far from solid. The intervention of C minor has given the reason for a startlingly beautiful change of key and has greatly increased the prospects of the movement as a whole.

Above the main theme floats its own inversion, and its second half is enriched by swelling trumpets, a sound of such splendid majesty as Bruckner rarely surpassed. As before there is a shift towards the dominant. This time it causes the biggest crisis of the movement. The integrity of the design is now at stake, and the B major-minor tendency has to be curbed. Therefore the end of the theme drifts into dark mysterious modulations; flute, clarinet, and basses are heard through high string *tremolandi*. This tilts the tonal balance in the opposite direction, so that Ex. 2 has to sound in an E minor that feels like the dominant minor of A minor. Its first 16 bars, newly scored, make the same (transposed) harmonic journey as before. From bar 335 (E major 6/3 chord) two successive waves rise strongly to the very threshold of B major. The challenge of B major is here so insistent that were Bruckner to state Ex. 4 in E minor it would certainly seem to be in the subdominant minor of B.

Originally Ex. 4 acted as the climax of a process. There is now no question of that, as it cuts in with a quiet sense of purpose in a startling G major. So the theme that so definitely confirmed the key of B on its first entry is now the decisive means of contradicting it; the impact of G major is a force that B major cannot withstand. Through C major, E flat, and G flat (which cannot now sound at all like F sharp!) Ex. 4 passes to A major, where it settles. There is a sudden *pianissimo* drop down to a low E, clearly the dominant of A (bar 391).

Here is the final masterstroke—A is to E as E was to B, so all Bruckner needs to do to restore E major is to state the whole of the main theme for the third and last time, letting it start this time in A major. It would automatically turn to E for the final blaze. But there is never anything automatic about Bruckner's reactions, especially in a work so mature as this. Instead he remembers that the expressive figure (b) from Ex. 1 has rarely been heard, and he makes it sweep in a grand arch over a dominant (E) pedal that slowly turns into a tonic. It is one of the finest and most memorable passages in the symphony, and it gives the composer the further advantage of reserving Ex. 1 (a) for the last climax, rearing nobly in E major, fully established for the first time since the beginning.

The plan of the first movement is thus divisible into two main parts, the first fostering the slow evolution of B minor and major out of a start that is not so much *in* as delicately poised *on* E major, and the second seeing the subtle resurgence of the true tonic, not without opposition from the pretender. When themes or thematic groups are restated their functions are cunningly changed. Ex. 1, instead of starting a process, becomes almost imperceptibly absorbed into one that began at bar 189, ninety-two bars earlier. Ex. 2, which at first was the means of pointing the way to B major, later causes the final attempt of that key to regain its sway (see the passage before letter T). Ex. 4, originally the signal for the victory of B, eventually defeats it by a sudden entry in G major and a modulation to A. Tovey was in a sense correct in remarking that "it is Bruckner's misfortune that his work is put forward by himself so as to present to us the angle of its relation to sonata form". But we must take care to examine the music from angles other than that we first notice, or the misfortune will be ours.

The *Adagio*, perhaps the most famous composition of Bruckner, is in C sharp minor, a key which the first movement, with all its range of tonality, avoids. This composer is always wonderfully circumspect in his use of tonality. C sharp minor is one of the keys most likely to occur in a piece in E major—yet its effect is carefully reserved for the slow movement. The opening is a vast paragraph containing, among others, the following three important elements:

Ex 5

Though the start is in C sharp minor, the tonality during this passage moves slowly towards F sharp minor, a big climax being poised upon its frontier. The *tutti* breaks off and a *diminuendo* leads solemnly to the second half of the expository part of the movement, settled serenely in F sharp major with a change of time and pace (*Moderato*) and a new theme of remarkable beauty:

Ex 8 (bar 37)

The mood of this heavenly episode was anticipated only once by Bruckner, in the *Adagio* of the First Symphony.* As it closes, the light fades, giving way to the funereal strains of Ex. 5, again in C sharp minor. At bar 85 the theme is deflected into F sharp, and the association of this key with recent happiness seems to evoke the slow rising passage that follows, since it is full of longing. It is based on Ex. 5 (a) and its inversion, and moves towards a crisis, heralded by urgent trumpet calls and reached at bar 101 with a striking turn to C major. This has a bearing on later events. With a softening of tone Ex. 6 follows in the new key, finely scored for flute and strings. More rising sequences involve a *crescendo* to the dominant of G. The expected G major is foiled by a statement of the whole of Ex. 6 (bar 114) beginning in E flat and leading naturally to A flat. Now comes a massive and typically Brucknerian *crescendo* based on successive terraces, in which Ex. 6 (a) enters in different keys and on different choirs of instruments. By way of A flat major, E major, F major and F sharp major, the long-delayed G major is attained in what is so far the weightiest climax of the movement (bar 127). G major, which sounds like the final stage in the sequence of keys initiated by E major at bar 121 (rising by semi-tones), now dies away revealing itself as the dominant of C. The suggestion of C, however, is but momentary, and the surprising appearance of Ex. 8 in A flat major shows that G major was not the end of the total chain. The *Moderato* has here a darker colouring and the theme is half concealed beneath a lovely new counterpoint (bar 133). It is soon clear that A flat major is simply G sharp major, the home dominant, from which impressive cloudy harmonies and hesitations drift back to C sharp minor.

The return of Ex. 8 in A flat, besides being a satisfying and necessary recapitulation, is thus a gigantic dominant preparation for the resumption of the tonic. Bruckner rarely repeats ideas for the purpose of mere symmetry, but makes them perform organic functions in living forms. His practice in the first movement is here carried further. He might well have given another statement of Ex. 6 (a) in A flat (= G sharp) at bar 128, moved at once to the tonic and written a complete (or slightly curtailed) restatement of Exx. 5 to 8 inclusive, following it by a suitable coda. This would have made a vast but obviously ungainly sonata-rondo, and would have been the sort of composition for which Bruckner is often blamed by cursory critics. But, as we shall soon see, a further repetition of Ex. 6 (a) in A flat would, apart from

* See p. 36.

its redundancy, ruin the still larger plan in the composer's mind.

The tonic brings back the main theme surrounded by flowing string figures. The complete Ex. 6 follows and mounts in one of Bruckner's greatest *crescendi*, growing with vast slowness into an awesome climax. Again, as in the earlier *crescendo* passage, a sequence of keys is employed, different and even more striking. From bar 164 onward it runs—F minor to A flat, F sharp minor to B flat, G sharp minor to A, D flat to E flat, and B major to the dominant of C sharp. Here the tension is immense. The G sharps in the bass change to A flats, and with a thrilling shock the music streams out in a shining C major. It is at this point that the disputed cymbal crash appears in the first published score of the symphony. The Seventh did not undergo such drastic revisions as some of its companions, but there are many minor discrepancies between the final autograph and the first printed edition, most of which may be safely put down to other hands. Haas removes the cymbal stroke and the parts for timpani and triangle at this place on the strength of a handwritten note *gilt nicht* (invalid) on the part; it is now disputed whether the writing is Bruckner's or not. There is no question that the three instruments were added as an afterthought at the suggestion of Arthur Nikisch, and there is also no question that the very similar effect at the corresponding place in the *Adagio* of No. 8 is authentic. Few who have been thrilled by the cymbal crash are likely to want to part with it, and I see no reason to do so—though I could be persuaded to do without the triangle, both here and in the Eighth.

It will be remembered that the previous high point in G major (bar 127) showed signs of leading to C, but was prevented from so doing by Ex. 8 in A flat. The present higher peak stands in brilliantly clear relation to the other, as also to the still earlier emphasis on C major (bar 101). But the final *dénouement* is to come. As the G major *tutti* was followed by a soft A flat major, so this C major shows itself in a similar light, and the quiet reaction is in D flat major, which is really C sharp, the tonic major. The marvellously controlled lingering *coda* is threefold. First, major turns to minor with a noble utterance of tubas and horns, based on Ex. 6 (a), cavernous and grand. Then follows Ex. 7, not heard since its first appearance, now no longer aspiring but ethereal and remote, floating high above a wonderful intermittent *pizzicato* bass C sharp. Last, Ex. 5 (a) emerges for the first time in the tonic major. The *coda* was not composed, as is often said, in memory of Wagner; it was, however, the thought that Wagner had not long to live that was its source. Anyone familiar with Bruckner's

Te Deum, written in the same period as the Seventh, will quickly recognize Ex. 6 as strongly resembling the *non confundar*.

The Scherzo is in A minor. Again Bruckner's strategy is effective, for this key, touched but once (and fleetingly) in the first movement and not at all in the *Adagio*, makes a strong impression. Significantly, the two other important keys in this third movement have previously had little prominence. C minor, in which the first stage of the Scherzo ends, has not been heard since its huge outbreak in the first movement, and F major, the key of the Trio, has hitherto existed only as an unobtrusive member of a few short key sequences. The freshness of the Trio, moreover, is made doubly sure by the strict exclusion of F major from the Scherzo, of which the succinct start states its complete thematic matter:

Ex 9

At bar 29 there is a quick shift to D flat, the first of a series of kaleidoscopic changes lasting for 24 bars. Then the dominant of C minor is reached (bar 53), and after some preparation C minor itself drives home a very massive climax. The absence of distinct first and second groups does not prevent this section from being a terse sonata exposition, as usual in Bruckner's scherzos. The development shows more swift modulations, beginning softly in A flat with (a) followed by (d). A repetition of this in G flat leads to inversions of (b) in A major, C sharp major, and E minor, the two latter keys being enmeshed in a

stretto by contrary motion. The strings are meanwhile busy with
derivatives of (a). Next come treatments of (d) and its companion (e).
Both these ideas become quite changed in character, passing through
many modulations, inversions, and contrapuntal combinations before
entering D flat, whence the trumpeting figure (b), in *stretto* with its own
inversion, careers to the home dominant. The first horn and subsequently
a trumpet display a free diminution of (b) (bar 165). The recapitulation,
coming after a hush (bar 185), is regular. Its first move is to B flat instead
of D flat, and the final climax thus fixes A minor. With all its breadth,
variety, and unity, this piece fills no more than four minutes.

The slower Trio, elegant and rich yet open-hearted, is in binary
form since its first part is incomplete, starting in F after some introductory drum taps and ending with a delightful surprise in D major.
The second part is begun by an inversion of Ex. 10 (a). Bruckner is
very economical, rarely leaving this phrase, and treating it with

Ex 10

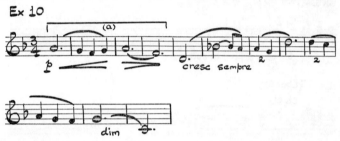

delicate resource. The return to F major finds the original melody
soaring before it finishes gently with flowing flute figures.

The Finale blends solemnity and humour in festive grandeur. It is
unique in form and difficult to describe despite the directness of its
address. The tonal organization is as subtle as it is everywhere else in the
symphony and, as in the first movement, the main theme foreshadows
by its modulation the key-system to follow:

Ex 11

This moves almost at once, as shown, from E to the key a major third higher, A flat. The next bar (10) cancels this by asserting E minor, whereupon the theme begins again in the dominant, B major. It now modulates with another *crescendo* to B flat, whence it starts once more. Then come two more steps to major mediants, B flat to D major, and D to F sharp major, leading to a bold progression which, rising, hits the dominant of G flat (G flat being really F sharp). All this sounds fearfully involved and academic, so we must observe that everything is in the highest of spirits. Before the music can settle in F sharp alias G flat, it subsides on to the dominant of F (bar 33). Instead of F major (or minor), however, there is a gorgeously modulating chorale, commencing in A flat major and thus consolidating the first change in Ex. 11 from E to A flat (this still makes aural sense even after all the intervening changes):

The chorale appears to modulate casually, but it is properly centred on A flat, which is soon confirmed by Ex. 13 in a return through the dominant of F. The resumption of Ex. 12 occasions a small rise in temperature that falls to the dominant of A. At this, the first *tutti* of the Finale bursts out in A minor with the following Herculean derivative of Ex. 11 (a):

A recurrence of this a semitone higher launches a great striding passage that stamps through F minor, B flat minor, A minor, and the dominant of D minor, culminating in two powerful brass fanfares on the successive dominants of G and A flat. It looks as if this cardinal stage is going to end with a climax in A flat, which is perhaps what we should expect in view of the modulation of Ex. 11 and the key of the chorale. Ex. 11 (b) does in fact enter in A flat, but its very nature compels it to rise to its major mediant, C major. After a short-lived effort by A flat to retake control (bars 117–27), the music dies away mysteriously in a C major that is not perfectly sure of itself, being not quite free from its earlier associations as the dominant of F (refer back to bar 33). Ex. 11 (b) is changed into a new figure:

Ex.15 (bar 133)

At present the three most important keys asserted have been (i) the tonic, E major, (ii) A flat major, and (iii) C major. They are clearly connected as a series of major mediants. Of the three, A flat has been most emphatic, E major least. Bruckner immediately illuminates the relationship by giving a soft free augmentation of Ex. 15 in A flat and repeating it at once in E major (bars 147–62). The threads are being drawn more closely. The tonic and its environs are now entered. At bar 163, in the subdominant minor, there is a humorously simple inversion of Ex. 11 ending in A major and overlapping with an equally playful inverted diminution of the chorale, whose second phrase is placed on the home dominant. Then Ex. 11 appears in E major in *stretto* by contrary motion, threaded by a quaver counterpoint. A tendency to strain after A flat is checked by a *crescendo*, and a second tremendous *tutti* on Ex. 14 makes a forcible entrance in the dominant minor. The counterstatement of its first phrase lands on the border of A flat (bar 198), for which the influence of the tonic now proves too strong. Its E flat becomes D sharp and the rest of the *fortissimo* stalks gigantically around home territories, crashing into a terrific unison on the dominant of E (the notation in flats does not deceive the ear). There is a silent pause.

The echoes of the titanic sound have scarcely died when the chorale begins in C major. The melody is so shaped that this time its second phrase modulates smoothly to F major. Strictly the third phrase would follow on the dominant of G, but it continues in F, thus emphasizing the original habit of C major to behave as the dominant of F. Any

pretensions C major might have had being nicely disposed of by this
tiny bit of dialectic, the theme becomes its old modulating self again
and Ex. 13 falls into the homely subdominant region of A major (over
a pedal E). Slight tension is raised by the intervention of the dominants
of F and A flat, but they are amiably kicked out by Ex. 11 (b) in A
major (bar 247). This is the start of what would be a mighty *coda* if
this amazing movement were neatly divisible. The theme, on the edge
of F sharp, is gloriously crowned by the brass (bar 251). It emerges
unscathed, travelling in the direction of A flat, and is swept up by
another thunderous *tutti*, driving towards the submediant. At bar 267
there is, perhaps, a reminiscence of the Fourth Symphony, blazing out
in E major. After a fiery contrapuntal combination in C sharp major
there is a furious hush and Ex. 11 leaps out in the tonic, which key is
now unmistakable. As at first it rushes to A flat, the brass crowning it
again; it restarts *for the first and only time* in A flat major, modulating
now to G (this corresponds to the move from B major to B flat in bars
11 to 19). The orchestra is wonderfully vivid as the theme flashes in
many brilliant shapes towards the home dominant; when it arrives
there the astonishing mass of tone is abruptly cut off. Then the main
theme, merging with Ex. 1 (a) (from which it is obviously derived),
resounds in the vast spaces of E major as, with golden fanfares, it rings
the final majestic climax.

It would be a pleasure to be able to answer the simple question
"What form is it in?" instead of having to describe this astounding
finale in such complicated narrative. But its unique organization is
describable only in its own terms and if we are to feel its immense
cogency and the utter originality of it we must give up the comforting
prop of any familiar yardstick. Many attempts have been made to
analyse this piece in conventional terms with "modified" this and
"telescoped" that, "truncated" this or "extended" that, all of them
laughable. The basis of the movement is the idea of major mediant
connections between keys, and the attempts of two competitors to oust
the rightful tonic. The form that grows from this is the resultant
of three tonal forces acting from different directions, one of them strong
enough to dominate the outcome, but not strong enough to maintain a
simple course by sweeping the others out of the way. The piece evolves,
and along no familiar lines, though the fact of key-conflict itself derives
from sonata. This and the first movement show a view of tonality that
foreshadows the profound achievements of a later symphonist, Nielsen,
in whom no trace of Bruckner's influence can be found.

The kind of structure we find in the Seventh benefits greatly from steadily maintained tempi, so that the evolution of the tonalities may unfold itself naturally and clearly, without distraction. This is especially true of the first and last movements, where the processes depend on a relatively undisturbed pulse; in both it is perfectly possible to find a main tempo from which deviations shall be no more than normal flexibilities, so that the basic rhythm is never lost. It is worth while mentioning the matter because there is some confusion between editions. Robert Haas, in preparing the first publication of the original in 1944, removed all performing instructions not unequivocally in Bruckner's hand. This resulted (particularly) in a first movement virtually in a single tempo and a finale similarly constituted and freed from the somewhat disruptive persistent *ritardandi* that, once having been applied to the tail-end of the main theme, recur with monotonous predictability in the earliest printing (Gutmann, 1885). Most of these amendments were restored by Leopold Nowak in his edition of 1954 on the grounds that they were "based undoubtedly on instructions"; in support of this theory Nowak quotes a letter from Bruckner to Nikisch saying "in the score there are many things of importance and frequent changes of tempo not noted". Nowak concludes that therefore "the enigma of these entries is solved . . . one of the very rare cases where in addition to the autograph, verbal instructions by Bruckner can and must be considered, because they are substantiated by letters".

It seems to me that no argument, however ingenious, can prove that specific tempo modifications at particular points in the score are authorized in detail by Bruckner's remark to Nikisch. For all we know he may have meant that he did not want metronomic rigidity, which would certainly destroy the expressiveness of the music. If Bruckner issued instructions to Joseph Schalk, where is the kind of evidence a purist musicologist ought to insist upon? It is surely impossible that such detailed instructions could have been merely verbal; if they were, we may be sure, knowing the Schalkian genius for re-interpreting Bruckner, that the instructions were not taken very literally. The verbal instructions assumed by Nowak might just as easily have taken place in some such conversation as this:

Schalk: You don't want absolutely rigid tempi, do you?
Bruckner: No, of course not.
Schalk: Right—leave it to us.

Such an exchange might have taken place before J. Schalk and Franz Zottmann played the first movement and Scherzo on two pianos in 1883 or when the same Schalk and Ferdinand Loewe played the whole symphony a year later. What these gentlemen did on the piano could very well be what we find in the Gutmann score (the proofs of which were read by Joseph) and in Nowak's "restoration". As always in such cases we must use our musical judgment: the structure shows (in my view decisively) that Haas acted correctly. The trouble with written tempo fluctuations is that they inevitably get exaggerated in performance; their presence in a case like this is more dangerous than their absence, for no sensitive conductor is going to march metronomically through Bruckner's music, while the insensitive ones will make grinding changes of gear at every apparently authorized excuse.

Not wishing to labour the point, I will mention but one especially pernicious example in the first movement, where the indications of the first edition can lead to an obscuration of the structure. In the Gutmann score (also in Nowak, Universal, and Eulenburg) the great C minor outburst at bar 233 is marked *molto animato*, and this usually leads to a violent acceleration of tempo that not only robs the passage of its majesty and spaciousness but also creates the problem of where and how to get back to the original quieter motion (for there is no cancellation indicated). Most conductors who observe this direction choose to return abruptly to the original speed at bar 281, obviously thinking thereby to emphasize an orthodox sonata recapitulation. But this is to share the delusions of those who complain that the movement as a whole is clumsy in its treatment of sonata. The real inevitability and flow of the process may be preserved only by getting rid of such automatic responses and by allowing the E major at bar 281 to float in unobtrusively, without the emphasis of a change of pace, to be confirmed gradually by everything that happens afterwards in the movement. The C minor passage gains enormously in both aptness and power if it is sustained by the main tempo, and what follows it then comes naturally.

CHAPTER IX

SYMPHONY No. 8, IN C MINOR

THE PREMIÈRE OF the Seventh Symphony on December 30th, 1884, under Nikisch in Leipzig was Bruckner's first taste of real success—significantly, outside Vienna, where he had received little but disappointment. He was sixty. In the following March Hermann Levi performed No. 7 in Munich, another notable triumph. Bruckner's satisfaction was complete when Ludwig II of Bavaria accepted the dedication. Even so, when the Vienna Philharmonic (which had not always been kind to him) wanted to follow these successes with a performance in Vienna, the composer begged them to refrain, for fear that the Viennese critics (and Eduard Hanslick in particular) would undo all the advantage gained in Germany. He was right concerning Hanslick; when the work was eventually done in Vienna in 1886 (under Richter) the enthusiasm of the audience did not prevent that egregious critic from describing the symphony as "sick and perverted", or from quoting such adverse comments as he could extract from German newspapers in the hope of dimming any impression that Bruckner had had a triumph in Germany. Hanslick's minions, Kalbeck and Dömpke, were positively abusive.* Bruckner would normally have been badly upset by such things, but his reputation was now growing in the outside world, the Seventh was being widely played, and he had the encouragement of several distinguished conductors who believed in his genius. Among these was Hermann Levi, whom he called *mein künstlerischer Vater*; what more natural than that Levi should be the first to see the score of the new Eighth, which Bruckner had finished in September 1887, after three years of work? And what could have been more shocking to the composer than Levi's rejection of it? Although the news was broken tactfully to him by Joseph Schalk, Bruckner was brought to a nervous crisis verging at times on mental breakdown.

Levi's sincerity is not in doubt. He certainly found the new symphony bafflingly different from the E major work he genuinely

---

* I am reminded of the *de haut en bas* attitude of some critics after a recent performance of Havergal Brian's magnificent Gothic Symphony, when a packed Albert Hall was the scene of one of the greatest standing ovations for many years.

loved, and failed to come to terms with it. In his defence it must be said that the score was not the one now known; it was the first version, still unpublished. Levi was not one of those who constantly badgered Bruckner to revise his music. He even warned him not to alter the First Symphony too much, and was full of praise for the Linz score of it. Nevertheless, this fright undoubtedly caused the revision of No. 8 in 1889–90, which included a new ending for the first movement, a completely new Trio, structural alterations in the *Adagio*, some cuts in the Finale, and considerable re-scoring. It is this version that must be regarded as definitive, though there are some dubious points that I shall discuss in the course of analysis: they concern the differences between the score published under Robert Haas's editorship in 1939 and that edited by Leopold Nowak and issued in 1955, both printed by the International Bruckner Society. Nowak has removed some passages which Haas included from the first version of 1887. From a purist musicological point of view Nowak's position is unassailable, but there are artistic reasons why the matter is worth discussing—these will emerge whenever we reach the relevant places in the symphony. We must be clear that Nowak's edition represents all that can be divined from Bruckner's own hand. Despite this (as we have learned only too well) we cannot be sure how much of what he wrote himself (or, more to the point, excised himself) is the result of external pressure. The demands of the musical structure must be our guide whenever we are not certain.

Within Bruckner's *ethos* (which is much wider in scope than is often supposed) one cannot find two works more contrasted than the Seventh and Eighth symphonies. No. 7 is poised and fundamentally relaxed, for all its tonal intricacy and originality; like the Second and the Fourth it is an expression of elevated content in the making of music. The sweeping dramatic force of the Eighth is almost new in Bruckner. No whole work anticipates its character, not even the Third, the most dramatically inclined of the earlier symphonies. The Fifth has an immense inner tension resembling that of Gothic architecture, and is dramatic as a totality rather than as a process; there is nothing in it that quite suggests the dark sense of crisis that fills the first movement of No. 8. The Eighth is the first full upshot of matters hitherto hidden in undercurrents and only intermittently allowed to erupt. But it eventually reveals its true background in the Finale, the background, in a sense, of Bruckner's life-work, a contemplative magnificence of mind beyond the battle. This Finale is not so much a victory over

tribulation as a state that had to be found behind it, slowly and sometimes painfully uncovered by the *Adagio*. But we shall come to that,
and must first go with Bruckner through the process of pacification
that results in its discovery.

It is to be well noted that the turbulent forces informing the first
movement compel Bruckner to final mastery of his own kind of newly
expanded sonata. Like all true and flexible artists, he bends method to
expressive purpose, and at his best he is consistent in so doing. The
main theme is given out in grim disquieting fragments:

The tonality is at first obscure, suggesting B flat minor (or even D
flat until the fifth bar), and the mystery is deepened until as late as bar
22, when an expected close in C minor is foiled by the *fortissimo* outburst of the opening F, now felt clearly as the subdominant of C. The

F

violent counterstatement reinforces the real tonic, C minor, with the drum, but it is not allowed to close in that key and it softens in the direction of A flat; the music falls, however, on to the home dominant, G major, at bar 51. The appearance of a beautiful new theme in Bruckner's characteristic mixed rhythm (derived from Ex. 1 (c)) insists that the ear accept for the moment G major as if it were an established key:

Ex 2 (bar 51)

This contains typical "passing keys" and swells out to an urgent pronouncement of G major (around bar 70). But its basis is not firm, and a new resumption of Ex. 2 has a different continuation, moving into the clouded region of E flat minor, where a new threat creeps; Mahler must have been strongly affected by this theme in the first movement of his Second Symphony:

Ex. 3 (bar 97)

The menace quickly flares into an extraordinary outbreak of jagged downward slashes athwart fiercely dissonant trumpet blares. They cease sharply, then a powerful *crescendo* culminates defiantly on the dominant of E flat major (bar 125). The massive fanfares abruptly die in vast spaces. A mysterious quiet, disturbed only by soft accents of the first theme, brings about the immensely dramatic and spacious end of the exposition in E flat major. The final resolution of the bass on to E flat comes after one of the longest and most breathtaking cadential preparations ever conceived (bars 125–39). Bruckner's masterly command of pace in this remarkable exposition should be appreciated. Without any alteration of tempo he contrives to compress his actively dramatic passages into short spaces, leaving himself the freedom to expand; so he need not sacrifice his profoundly characteristic deliberation and breadth, even in a sonata movement of such disquiet as this.

So broad a preparation for E flat means that it must not be left too soon. Accordingly, Bruckner stays rooted in it for no less than twenty-five bars of extreme hush, and long-drawn augmentations of Ex. 1 (b) hang in the dark air. The obscurity grows with a turn to the minor and then, with a soft move into G flat (marked by a striking entry of of the contrabass tuba) the development begins at bar 165. Augmentations and inversions of Ex. 1 (b) persist, proceeding with great majesty from key to key. The harmony is of considerable originality, creating dissonances of fearsome smoothness as it finds the full power of the brass. All at once the sound disappears on the dominant of G flat (bar 192); in G flat comes an inversion of Ex. 2. It does not stay there; after a slight rise in tension it slips very suddenly into intense *pianissimo* preparation on the home dominant (bar 201). The recapitulation can already be felt at a distance. This is not to say that its form is predictable; as we shall find out, Bruckner marks it with one of his greatest strokes.

It will be remembered that the movement began in an alien tonality and that although C minor was strongly thrust forward by the first group, that key was never permitted to form any kind of conclusive cadence. Power of suggestion was enough to impress C minor on the mind as the real basis of the passage. Bruckner now recognizes the clamouring fact that a full, sufficiently spacious and unequivocal dominant preparation is the only thing that can restore the home tonic firmly enough to balance and efface the vastly comprehensive establishment of E flat at the end of the exposition. Presumably that is his object as he now settles down to one of his own peculiarly cumulative dominant *crescendi*, with an inversion of Ex. 2 in the violins, punctuated by Ex. 1 (a) deep in the bass at shortening intervals (bar 205 *et seq.*). No simpleton of the type sometimes portrayed as Bruckner could have thought of the music as far as this point. Few geniuses, and only the subtlest of these, could have thought of the stroke that now follows. Having reached this dominant *crescendo*, most composers would have been satisfied to reinstate C minor by means of the growing excitement, with a plain (and probably impressive) statement of Ex. 1 at the height of the climax, perhaps expanded in some way and almost certainly chained to the tonic by a pedal, for it is by nature a modulating theme. No doubt to point triumphantly to the essential banality of such a scheme is to be wise after the event—but how, after such an event as Bruckner's, can anyone be anything but wise? He allows the dominant preparation to go on for 11 bars, and then the bass (Ex. 1 (a)) starts to rise by semitones. The violins slip weirdly from their pitch and the horns become articulate (bar 212). In five bars the music heaves bewilderingly: then it finds a grip at bar 217 *on the dominant of B flat minor*. The rising tumult sweeps in Ex. 1 (b) in the bass, augmented and titanic, in precisely the same tonal position as at the start of the symphony, now combined with a free augmented inversion of Ex. 2 to make a colossal irruption of sound. Three times this mighty combination rears itself; at the end of the third and most powerful upheaval there is an abrupt *pianissimo*, with C minor fully established.

What is the real point of this tremendous passage? In effect the composer says: "My main subject is a modulating one—it begins on the dominant of B flat minor and moves chromatically to C (Ex. 1 (b)). If I were to recapitulate it in C minor, I would have to do one of two things: (i) I could start it on the note G, whence it would move to D, which could then be treated quite simply as the fifth of the dominant chord, falling naturally by step to C, or (ii) I could flatten out the whole theme into a mere rhythm without any kind of tonal ambiguity and with plenty of elemental power. Of the two suggestions I would prefer (i) since it is the more musically interesting: but it is unsatisfactory because it fails to ram home what I wanted to show at the outset, that the turn from B flat minor to C is not a full establishment of C minor, in spite of its impressiveness. If I were to shift the theme up a tone, I could without difficulty keep it within the bounds of C minor, as already argued, but I should lose its most precious attribute, its tonal restlessness. Why not make as if to bring about C minor by dominant preparation and then undermine the whole idea by slipping on to the old dominant of B flat minor, blazing out the theme in its original form (augmented to increase its breadth)? It will then move to its C, which will demand further confirmation and thus urge me to state the theme in immense steps until it crashes over *upon the dominant of C*, leaving no more doubt about the tonality. Three such statements should be enough, the middle one increasing the tension by being a minor third above the first, and the third relieving it by being poised gigantically on the home dominant. I shall thus have made the needed dominant preparation with far more power and incident than if I had been content with my first notion."

Whether or no Bruckner actually reasoned thus with himself (more likely his intuitive genius took a short cut through any such chain of arguments), this magnificent tripartite passage flings the shadow of C minor across the 53 bars that succeed it. When it ceases, a solitary flute

is left hovering over a drum pedal on C with faint cavernous sounds
of the last four notes of Ex. 1 (b) in the bass; between these extremes
soft trumpets enter with the bare rhythm of Ex. 1 (b) on the tonic.
Thus Bruckner makes a more telling use of this device (the reduction
of Ex. 1 (b) to its rhythm) than if he had relied upon it for the previous
climax. The bass figure slides into the upper strings and initiates
another *crescendo*, curving up into a great wave, through which the
trumpet rhythm may still be discerned. The reaction from this is a
quiet counterstatement of a new form of the main theme in oboe
(bar 282), clarinet (bar 286), and trumpet (bar 290), with a flickering
flute and string *tremolando* accompaniment (the oboe has the very form
of Ex. 1 (b) that Bruckner refrained from using in the most obvious
place, the form beginning on the note G; here it is carefully hidden for
a reason that will appear very much later in the symphony). At bar 29
the strings burst out with the last phrase of the theme, much as they did
at bar 18, thus confirming the unity of the whole enormous expansion
of the first group from bar 224 to 302. During this subdued counterstatement (which contrasts with the loud one of the exposition) there
are apparent modulations; they do not affect the issue, and would
better be called inflexions.

As before, the expected close in C minor is turned into an alien
dominant, which now moves unexpectedly into the familiar region of
E flat and a fresh version of Ex. 2. After so spacious a design only a full
recapitulation of the second group is possible. Like Schubert, Bruckner
gives it with its thematic material largely unchanged, but with different
key-relationships. By this means he creates symmetry without
tautology. He also gives the restatement of the second group a new
meaning, for it is now part of the restoration of C minor, even though
it begins in E flat; the fact is grimly confirmed by the apparition of
Ex. 3 at bar 341, in C minor. The tonic cannot now be undermined.
The fierce sequel leads directly to the *coda*, where is the most minatory
of all Bruckner's climaxes. The rhythm of Ex. 1 (which is, incidentally,
the same as that of the first theme of Beethoven's Ninth Symphony)
cuts remorselessly through the surging mass of the orchestra and the
most chilling moment is its sudden isolation on the brass, with nothing
but a thunderous drum far below it. At the end comes prostration,
collapse; broken wisps of the main theme drift blackly out. Bruckner
called this *coda* a "death watch", and for once his description is apt;
it is the most frightening music he had yet imagined. The original first
movement ended *fortissimo*, like all such by this composer; the change

converted the piece into the greatest of its type since Beethoven's *Coriolan* overture.

After human tragedy comes mysterious and titanic energy. For the first time Bruckner places the Scherzo second in a symphony. If he really wished to create here a portrait of the indomitable, clumsily obstinate figure of *Deutscher Michel* (as he said), he completely dwarfed it with music whose fantastic power suggests nothing so much as the constant thud of a colossal celestial engine beyond even Milton's imagining. The brilliantly imaginative use of string *tremolandi* gives the sound a keen and chimerical glitter, and the trenchant main theme pounds with the continuous reciprocating action of a mighty piston:

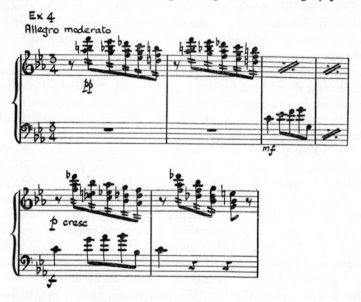

Like all Bruckner's scherzos this one (in C minor) is in a concentrated sonata form without clearly defined first and second groups, and with a development of comparatively reflective nature. The exposition ends with a climax in E flat major, after which the main theme is inverted *legato*, passing through a wide range of harmony and key, and giving rise to much fine woodwind writing. The recapitulation is caused by a settling on the home dominant (over a tonic drum pedal) and the horn entry that began the movement. The final sledgehammer climax is thrown into C major by a single change of harmony in the restatement (compare bars 37 and 171). A stupendous piece—and its overwhelming force is generated as much by the formidable regularity of its phrasing as by its actual theme or the weight and perfect clarity of its orchestration.

The Trio is a notable slow movement in itself, and its calmness is a relief—the first period of genuine rest in the symphony so far. Its refreshing quality is enhanced by the fact that its key, A flat major, has not previously been established in either the first movement or the Scherzo. It is also a compressed sonata scheme without separable groups of themes, the exposition ending in E major, another tonality that has hitherto been avoided. For the first time in his career Bruckner uses harps, which he treats with delicate care; the almost French fastidiousness of the scoring in bars 33–44 should be observed—yet the music is innately Austrian. The recapitulation comes at bar 61 after a succinctly expressive return through four solemn detached phrases, and has a finely calculated alteration of key-relationships. The last gentle restoration of A flat is achieved, with exactness and poetry, only in the last nine bars. After this the Scherzo is even more impressive.

The highest tribute to Bruckner's power of subtle composition need do no more than point out that the coherence of so immense a piece as the *Adagio* of this symphony hangs to a great extent on a single chord. This chord, moreover, is heard no more than four times during the full length of the movement. It is not even an unusual chord, but a 6/3 triad. Such an assertion looks like hyperbole, but analysis shows that without this chord, unobtrusively used though it is, the most important passage (and consequently the whole plan) would lose its thread.

D flat major is the key of the *Adagio*. Like the keys of the Trio, it has barely been touched upon earlier in the work and so is new to the ear. The first theme, over faintly pulsing chords, has a strange air of troubled detachment; the two phrases shown in Ex. 5 appear in the first ten bars:

Ex. 5 (bar 3)

Extremely important is the persistent D flat (becoming C sharp) in
the bass. It is intended to penetrate the mind, for it causes a compelling
harshness, almost coarseness, that characterizes the first *fortissimo* chord,
underlying a loud aspiring phrase (bar 15). This is a 6/3 chord of A
major, with its root (the third, the C sharp) heavily doubled in the bass.
Now the most elementary student of harmony knows that a doubled
third, especially in the bass, results in an unpleasant roughness: one may
therefore be pardoned for wondering why Bruckner has been at pains
to double and redouble in the lower brass this dangerous note. The
answer is that he wants this chord to be peculiarly recognizable without
being complex or abstruse, as later events prove.

Ex 6 (bar 15)

The reply to this is a marvellously sonorous string passage; joined by
the brass, it rises to a seraphic series of chords for strings and harp,
resting at length on F major (bar 28). As if nothing had happened, the
opening D flat harmonies are heard again, and Ex. 5 (a) returns. Before
(b) can follow, the harmony changes to B major and once more Ex. 6,
with its singular scoring, asserts itself, now a tone higher than before.
Its noble sequel, duly transposed, ends now on a chord of G major
(bar 45). As the F major of bar 28 dropped a major third back to D
flat, so we expect this G major to fall to E flat, especially if we know
that the drop of a major third between tonalities is a favourite sound
with Bruckner. That this does not now happen is another important
factor in the cogency of the movement as a whole. Instead, an intervening horn leads to one of Bruckner's most beautiful ideas, beginning
in E major (Ex. 7).

As will be seen, the chief characteristic of this superb theme lies in its
tonal freedom, its refusal to be bound by any one key: its second
statement, starting again from E, moves to B minor instead of the
original F minor, and then leads to a profoundly calm tuba theme,

Ex 7 (bar 47)

sounding remote depths as it passes from C major into F (bar 67). This second section of the *Adagio* closes peacefully in G flat at bar 81, whence a 14-bar link, composed of expressive woodwind derivatives of Ex. 7, drifts back to D flat and the opening theme. The tonality throughout the second group has been made purposely kaleidoscopic, for the composer is determined that D flat shall be the only key to have firm entrenchment; the effect at the end of the whole *Adagio* is that the tonic has never lost its hold. The very fact that G flat is the home subdominant, rather than the dominant, makes the return to the tonic as inevitable as if it were in a *coda*.

The renewal of the opening material brings about a very slow, widely modulating *crescendo*, based entirely on Ex. 5 (a) and (b). As the dynamics increase, the mood becomes gloomier, as if a fruitless search is in progress; the climax is approached with a certain dogged persistence that may not appeal to less patient ears. For once the owners of such ears have my very real sympathy, for it must be confessed that so far as the raising of climaxes in this great movement is concerned, Bruckner has burdened himself with a disadvantage in the nature of both (a) and (b) of Ex. 5, (a) being virtually a flat straight line, and (b) a descending phrase of perilously languishing character, replete with *appoggiature*, and rhythmically not really strong enough to be transformed by inversion. Neither has innate kinetic energy, both bear down oppressively on the spirit and (b) climbs laboriously when inverted; one can interpret the fact positively or negatively according to sympathy or lack of it. To me it seems that the growth towards its climaxes of the *Adagio* of No. 7 is more inevitable, simply because the thematic material generates of itself the natural requisite tensions.

Nevertheless, there is the undeniable fact that the *crescendo* we are now considering rises to a heavily obstinate attack on a 6/4 chord of B flat (bar 125), then expires plaintively *without finding the clinching matter of Ex. 6*. So its stubborn dolefulness is not without artistic justification, and its real character may be appreciated only in the light of the whole movement. The falling phrases lead now to the second appearance of Ex. 7 and its train, beginning in E flat, with an effect doubly radiant after the gloom from which it rises.

The significance of this E flat is simply that it is the very key in which we expected the second group to begin at bar 47, when the music had paused on a G major chord that had, it seemed, every reason to fall a major third. If Bruckner defeats expectations it is usually because he has some long-term reason, and if the term is too long for some listeners, this is understandable; but the limiting factor is certainly not Bruckner's. Phenomena such as this have their effect, as we have observed before, even on the listener who knows not why. The second group emerges almost complete: it is surely remarkable that this section, apart from the *coda* the most serene part of the movement, is tonally the most mobile. The orchestration is now enriched in various ways, the end of the group truncated, and a new wistful continuation forms a fine-drawn link to yet another return of the main theme in the tonic. Now follows the crux of the whole.

As so often with the opening of a Bruckner passage designed to create the last climax, the theme is now accompanied by a movement of semiquavers and a number of more fragmentary embellishments, some highly expressive. The tension begins to grow and at bar 197 the attention is powerfully caught by a *fortissimo* 6/3 chord of C major, its E thickly, almost grotesquely, reinforced in the bass. At last, we think, comes Ex. 6, for this is unmistakable. But it is merely the beginning of a masterly delaying process and this one chord is repudiated by a quick hush and some rising Brucknerian brass chords. Four bars later comes another identically balanced 6/3 chord of E, its G sharp heavily underlined at its root: the tension is doubled when this, too, is silenced by a similar hush. A *crescendo* brings about a crashingly urgent outburst of Ex. 5 (a).

At this juncture occurs the first of the cuts apparently made by Bruckner, the passage having been restored by Haas from the first version. It is a short one, but more than interesting. In the Haas score the *ff* statement of Ex. 5 (a) at bar 205 is interrupted by another *pianissimo*, based on Ex. 5 (b), which seems to be drifting when it is suddenly obliterated by a precipitate assault of Ex. 6, the long-awaited subject, but on a 6/4 (not a 6/3) chord of A flat. The clearer dominant sound of the 6/4 suggests that a release is in sight, but it comes too suddenly itself to provide a climax; it therefore gives way to a resumption of the soft derivatives of Ex. 5 (b). It is the *pianissimo* (bars 209–18 in the Haas score) that Bruckner cut out, so that the outburst of Ex. 6 follows directly the loud entry of Ex. 5 (a). Thus, because of the cut, Ex. 6 is turned into a premature climax instead of a dramatic interrupting anticipation of things to come, and because it presumes to be the climax, there is no sense in its petering out, which had so much significance in the original. In the cut version the continuation of Ex. 6 is made to sound like a mere excuse to prolong the movement, a clear example of the way in which a cut, whether made by the composer or not, can actually increase the *longueurs* of a piece of music, defeating its own object. Haas, in my view, though his practice was not musicologically ethical, showed real insight in restoring the passage, which is vital to the organic growth of the whole complex.

The *piano* is resumed in E major (Haas, bar 221, Nowak, 211), and two more *crescendi*, with gathering excitement, bring about the real climax, a hugely expansive augmentation of Ex. 6, on a 6/4 chord of E flat, shifting majestically on to a massive chord of C flat (H. bar 253, N. 243). It is worthy of note that in the first version of the symphony this climax was not in E flat, but in C major; it might be thought that Bruckner changed it because the C major may have sounded too much like the climax of the *Adagio* of No. 7, but I suspect that the deeper reason lies in the fact that E flat bears a clear relation to the B flat at bar 125, in much the same way as the final C major climax in the Seventh's *Adagio* is related to the earlier high point in G major.

It should now be plain that the whole of this process would be impossible without the peculiarly recognizable constitution of the chord of Ex. 6, and it says much for Bruckner's grasp of detail (when he is not put off his stroke by pressure to revise) that so vast a plan can be pivoted on so simple a device. He is able to arouse expectations by the severely economical use of a single chord (and an ordinary diatonic one at that), heard only four times in the huge movement, but each time suggesting the theme for which the music seems to be searching, and so raising the tension. Having invoked its power of suggestion, he then makes no further use of it, founding the climax itself on a clearer and simpler 6/4 chord, and relying on the theme itself to enforce the point. At the end of the last *fortissimo* there is a small detail in the revision which ought to be adhered to if the Haas score is performed: Haas cuts off the full orchestra all at once, leaving the harp high and dry—the revision protects the harpist from this embarrassment and the listener from acute discomfort by sustaining the violins until the harp has finished its *arpeggio* (H. bar 253, N. 243).

To increase the sense of symmetry and release, Ex. 6 is succeeded by its original chorale-like continuation and the soaring string and harp passage is now intensified. After this comes the *coda*, perfectly balanced and inimitable in its Brucknerian solemnity, essentially a long horn solo that forms a new and amazingly broad melody from Ex. 5 (a), with soft asides in the violins. In performance the top horn line should be brought out and the strings subdued. I suggest this in the face of the markings in all editions of the score, which reverse the situation, when the over-prominent violin phrases are apt to seem repetitive, obscuring the real *melos*. The end dissolves quietly into a slow descending scale that, while it soothes away the strains and efforts, even mortifications, of some parts of the movement, yet is subtly inconclusive. The tensile strength of this *Adagio* is much taxed by stress between the nature of the themes of Ex. 5 and the climax building in which they are made to participate (they cannot dominate it). The dangers can be aggravated by too slow a tempo, which places an unendurable weight on the shoulders of Ex. 5 (a)—unfortunately one hears this nearly always. Schubert's *Der Wanderer*, which has virtually the same theme, may be taken as slowly as the artists can or dare, for it is entirely brooding; no energy is required for large-scale climaxes, as it is in this movement. Not that any Bruckner *adagio* should ever be hurried; usually a courageous slowness brings the most rewards. Here, however, the themes themselves do not permit it, as Bruckner well knew when he added the proviso *doch nicht schleppend* (but not dragging).

The Finale is, for all its splendour, the calmest part of the symphony. It is the cathedral the architect has been trying, through all the world's distractions, to find in his mind's eye. One by one the impediments have been removed, until the image is clearly revealed. It can now be contemplated, sometimes with quiet absorption, sometimes with a sense of exhilaration, and once recalling past despair. Again we must not expect such a finale to develop speed; its movement is vast and slow, and its active periods do not affect the deep pulse that informs its life. Pauses and inaction have their rightful place in its massive delibera-tions, and it is a grave mistake to suppose that the structure is weakened by them; they are the open spaces in the cathedral. Stillness prevails whenever the proportions demand it, and Wagner's dictum that "composition is the art of transition" does not apply, at least not if one assumes that composition consists entirely of notes. The longer I know this movement, the more authoritative does it seem in every bar, and the more sure am I that it is the greatest part of the work. In it Bruckner finds the essence of his own nature.

The magnificent paean with which the brass celebrate the occasion is modulatory. It opens out over a strong rhythm on F sharp, which is really G flat in relation to the previous *Adagio*, but quickly shows that D flat major is still the key:

It is as if Bruckner is acknowledging that the peace of mind achieved at the end of the *Adagio* has made it possible to see clearly the way ahead. The theme now rises by the same means as before to E flat (bar 25), from where it is a short step to the tonic C minor. Here there is a new incisive phrase:

Now there is a descent of great beauty and dignity (with a wonderful flash of colour from trumpets and horns at bar 40) to a soft, glowing close in C major, the rhythm of the strings fading out at bar 67. Characteristically Bruckner begins a new theme without intervening harmony, in A flat major, with his favourite drop in tonality of a major third. It is a noble idea with two simultaneous elements, of which (b)

proves to be the more important, and a third (c) which is capable of transformation:

Ex. 10 (bar 69)

The music is purged of all the disturbed, romantic harmony that sometimes impeded the search of the *Adagio* for peace. It is simple and clear, with great purity of line that is in no way affected. A really romantic composer can contrive a curiously cloying and sentimental result from the use of "pure" diatonics in contrast with lush chromaticism. Not so Bruckner, who maintains throughout this Finale a just and classical equilibrium between diatonic and chromatic harmony. Ex. 10 (c), at bar 75, descending by conjunct motion, should be noticed; not only does it have special consequences much later, but it immediately gives rise to an expressive string passage which was cut out of the first publication in 1892 (this can be found in both Haas and Nowak, bars 93–98). This passage bears a slight resemblance to a few bars in the first movement of the Seventh Symphony (bars 197–201). The analytical powers of Joseph Schalk may perhaps be assessed from a letter he wrote to Max von Oberleithner in 1891 complaining that this "reminiscence of the Seventh" seemed to him "quite unfounded"! Haas and Nowak are both right to restore it; in this case it certainly looks as if the excision were made at the instigation of Joseph, but Nowak keeps the truncation in the similar place before Oo which also sounds like a Schalkism (compare bars 584–98 in Haas with bars 564–6 in Nowak). The small and natural climax made each time by this clear extension of Ex. 10 (c) is necessary for spacious proportions as well as for symmetry. Further derivatives follow sequentially on the tubas. Then a return to Ex. 10 (a + b), more fully scored, causes a change to the dominant of E flat, through G flat, during which the first four notes of Ex. 10 (b) turn into a new shape in the bass:*

* Bar numbers attached to the music examples now refer to the Haas edition.

The music begins to sound mysterious, and soon the determined
solemn march of the crotchets of Ex. 11 creates a new theme in E flat
minor:

It breaks off, giving way to another offshoot of Ex. 10 (c), momentarily in C sharp minor, then on the dominant of D minor. In D

minor it is joined by the rhythm of Ex. 11, and the steady crotchet
motion passes to the bass as the key then changes to G flat with new
melodic invention in the violins. G flat is only the relative major of E
flat minor, and inevitably there comes a powerful *tutti* on the dominant
of E flat, now solidly secure, animated by the crotchet movement and
spelling out the rhythm of Ex. 8 (bar 183). In the first version of the
symphony this leads to a fine 20-bar cadential passage that wheels
beautifully down to E flat major. I cannot believe that Bruckner
willingly sacrificed this, and strongly approve of Haas's restoration of
it; the feeble four bars of drum and *pizzicato* substituted have nothing
to recommend them musically and spoil the proportions. Again Haas's
instinct is correct, even if he offends the more scientific musicologists.
From now on we shall have to distinguish between his and Nowak's
bar numbering, for the latter editor punctiliously retains the alteration,
it being in Bruckner's handwriting. The enormously long-drawn close
in E flat major that follows is one of those sublimely static periods we
have mentioned; its vast amplitude must be felt in relation to the

design as a whole. The revision slightly shortens it, and Haas (again with the right instinct for proportion) puts back the original (compare H. bars 253-8 with N. 237-8).

We have now reached the end of the first stage. It can, if you insist, be called the exposition so long as normal sonata processes are not expected. The tonic of the movement, C, has so far been emphasized only at the end of the first paragraph, and that was a long time ago. So it must be found again, and the rest of the movement carries out the kind of search that we observed in the first movements of the Fifth and Seventh Symphonies, the gradual achievement of the tonic in stages, with recapitulatory elements occurring in the course of establishing symmetry rather than being associated with the dramatic tonal returns of sonata. The awakening from the intense quiet is very gradual. First, Bruckner muses upon Ex. 13, modulating to G flat (H. bar 285, N. bar 265), where its inversion begins the bass to a long reflective *cantilena*. This becomes impassioned and returns to E flat minor, where motion is felt once more with a soft entry of the inversion of Ex. 12 (letter U, both editions). The determined rhythm of this theme now commands the course of the music and brings about a massive statement of Ex. 9 (still in E flat minor), which now has a new kind of familiarity, explained by its melodic similarity to Ex. 13 and its forbears, to which it is now related (another "promoted" derivative of the type we noted in the Scherzo of the Fifth Symphony).* Ex. 12 is combined with it. There are three such impressive combinations, the first two separated by a *piano* development of Ex. 12, and each a tone above the other, like great rock terraces; the last, beginning at letter Y (both scores), rests grandly on the home dominant.

Instead of the expected tonic, however, there is a new soft development of Ex. 8, one of Bruckner's most original inspirations, a soft fine web of delicate sound, modulating spaciously through foreign harmony, sequentially at first, later rising in tension and breaking off from a diminished chord (H. bar 406, N. bar 386). The last powerful *tutti* ended on the home dominant (letter Z, both scores), and as if the shadow of this has not yet gone, a quietly purposeful paragraph (still developing Ex. 8) now starts in C major: a definite attempt to reinstate the tonic. But the time is not yet ripe for that; the keys begin to shift again, enlivened by manifold products from Ex. 12, ranging as far as A major and G flat before settling down darkly on the dominant of A minor (Dd in both versions). Suddenly the trumpets stab out with

* See p. 116.

the repeated F sharps that began the movement and, since this passage was originally the means of fixing C, it at once infers the possibility of a return to the tonic. The main theme, once more majestic on the brass, drives forward powerfully through new sequences, finally completing itself in A flat (Ff in both scores): is this the resolution? Not quite; another series of short and urgent upward steps finally reach C major with terrific force (H. bar 495, N. bar 475). A threefold *fff* accentuation of this key releases enough energy to drive the music with high impetus for 58 bars, during which it moves around C major-minor, sweeping over one huge apex and halting abruptly at the height of a second (Ll in both scores). All this is based on Ex. 8. The tonic has now been asserted more strongly than ever before.

The dissonance on which this passage culminates at Ll is left on the horns, which seem to be blowing across a great gulf. It softens, apparently in the direction of A major, but at the last moment the dominant seventh of A is treated as a German sixth in A flat—and in that key the calm strains of Ex. 10 begin to flow again. This is a stroke of genius. Bruckner is often able to make completely new use of recapitulated material; here he does so, but merely by recalling it in the same key as before! The first time (bar 69) the A flat major is a turn in a new direction, a reaction from the first postulate of C, the beginning of a long process towards other regions. Here, coming after a long and vehement development that stayed in C minor-major, and being approached by a modulation rather than a plain silence, it has the effect, not of going away, but of coming home, of confirming C minor by behaving simply as its submediant. Bruckner does not even have to do much more than alter the scoring here and there for the sake of added freshness, and the quiet depth of the music is the perfect relief after the immense and complex stretch that has passed. The end of the paragraph is abbreviated and turns naturally to C minor for Ex. 12.

The next incident, in a symphony of masterstrokes, should perhaps be accounted the grandest and subtlest of them all. When Ex. 12 first appeared it was eventually followed by a forcible formal *tutti*, based on the rhythm of Ex. 8 (bar 183). Now the last re-entries Ex. 10 and Ex. 12 have given a sorely needed sense of symmetry to a design already stretched as far as human imagination is able: this symmetrical impression must be confirmed. A statement of the *tutti* just mentioned would undoubtedly serve that purpose in a conventional way, but would hardly be worthy of its adventurous context. What actually happens is a superb illustration of the way Bruckner thinks in terms of balanced masses and voids rather than recapitulated themes or sections in sonata-type music. His first impulse is that a big *tutti* is required (not so big that it endangers the success of the final *coda*, but big enough to counterweigh its distant predecessor). How can this be done without stiffness? Why not both effect this balance and drive home the point of the whole symphony at a blow? And so he hits on the idea of rising to a crisis, at the heart of which, grimmer than ever, shall appear the theme of the first movement: there is his required *tutti*, and there is the supreme question for his *coda* to answer. Many composers have hit upon this sort of recall as a purely emotional device, but how many would have made the theme grind into the score in this form?

Ex 14 (bar 652)

It is the very form of the subject that Bruckner refrained from using at the *reprise* of the first movement, that starting on the note G, the form in which it is most surely kept within C minor's grip. Its only previous appearance (oboe, first movement, bar 282) was carefully concealed and redirected, like the composer's original scores, "for fifty years' time". Such foresight is uncanny, and is the kind of stroke that distinguishes Bruckner from the type of composer whose weakness is, in Tovey's words, "where the ghosts of former movements seem to be summoned . . . to eke out his failing resources". After the turmoil has subsided, the final climax is evolved with the greatest possible dignity and grandeur; the *coda* begins at Uu in both editions. As with most of Bruckner's ultimate passages, it opens in darkness, breathing upon dim fragments of the main theme, passing from key to key as it climbs in a long *crescendo*. The strings persist in smoky figurations that burst into flame as the burning sun touches them; the last triumphant affirmation of C major is the complete reply to everything, and it contains elements of the main themes of all four movements. The end is abrupt but of tremendous finality.

CHAPTER X

SYMPHONY No. 9, IN D MINOR
(unfinished)

IN THE WHOLE of Bruckner's life there were but two periods in which he may be said to have experienced something like full creative confidence, the early period of the D minor and E minor masses and the First Symphony (1864-6) and an eight-year span between 1875 and 1883, during which the Fifth, Sixth and Seventh Symphonies were written, as well as the String Quintet. As we have seen, these are the fully mature works which underwent least revision (the Quintet actually gave him more trouble in this respect than the symphonies, but only because he was using an unfamiliar medium). Levi's failure to accept the Eighth brought back all his old fears and must have sparked off the compulsive revising of his last years, which completely disrupted his agonized struggles to compose the Ninth. Even if we did not know the circumstances in which his last work was attempted, the self-doubt, the ill health, and even (I suspect) an ebbing away of the religious faith that had hitherto protected him from even worse psychological wounds than he had already suffered, the torso of the Ninth Symphony would itself be evidence of travail. And the evidence lies, not only in the hitherto unequalled dimensions of the work (which, had it been completed, would have been bigger than the Fifth or the Eighth), but in the very nature of the music itself, often dark to the pitch of black-ness, and rent with such anguish as he had until now almost succeeded in keeping out of his music. There is tragedy in the first movement of the Eighth, objectively expressed, and there are more than a few examples in Bruckner's work of various kinds of conflict—the Fifth is a mighty battleground, but it is like some great classical fresco, and if we turn to the strange and compelling tonal conflicts of the last movement of the Sixth, we do not have the feeling that the composer is himself terrified by his own fantasies. But in the Ninth we sometimes receive this impression, not so much in the ferocious Scherzo as in parts of the first movement and large tracts of the tormented *Adagio*.

At first, studying the vast mass of sketches for the Finale (many fully or extensively scored), I used to think that the completed movement would have resolved the tensions of the symphony by revealing an

essentially calm and majestic mind behind all the emotional disturbances of the rest; but the more familiar are these sketches, the more
marked does the impression become that the subjective elements are
still overwhelmingly there, that Bruckner's condition was not such
as to be able to exorcize them. It was clear in the Eighth that the
Finale performed precisely this function after the troubled uncertainties
of feeling in the *Adagio* and, as we have seen, Bruckner's tendency in
his mature last movements has so far been to disclose a mental background that cannot easily be disturbed by outward events. This is a
matter we have discussed before, and which the next chapter will
mention again. In the meantime I must confess to more than scepticism
about attempts to complete the Ninth Symphony, not only because
the final *coda* is altogether missing (and it would be a bold, not to say
impertinent, man who would try to compose Bruckner's greatest
climax for him) but because the sketches do not provide the
momentum to support such a *coda*. Alfred Orel has skilfully assembled
a conflation of them into a more or less continuously written four-
stave score, and others have made full scores 400-odd bars long, relying
in part on the instrumental indications shown by Bruckner. But from
the sketches one can divine only broad outlines; it is possible to
identify developmental and recapitulatory elements, but there is no
real inner continuity perceptible as an organic process, no genuine
coherence, and often a total absence of those inner parts that normally
mean so much to the growth of a Bruckner movement. Details of this
nature cannot be satisfactorily invented on the required scale by anyone
but the composer himself; if the ideas in the sketches themselves were
organically continuous, the problem of filling out details would be
formidable enough, but the fact that they are not makes the task
impossible. I do not believe that anyone will ever succeed in doing for
this movement what Deryck Cooke has done so magnificently for
Mahler's Tenth Symphony. There is no doubt that Mahler saw his
Tenth whole. Bruckner was still trying to conceive the exact form and
nature of his finale.

In the last two years of his life Bruckner did nothing but wrestle
with these sketches and his ultimate inability to resolve the ideas into a
whole was almost certainly due to a failing health that was mental as
well as physical. This is not to suggest that his mind was breaking
down; he had always been subject to acute nervous disorders and could
easily be thrown off balance. Redlich★ gives an account of his various

★ *Bruckner and Mahler* (J. M. Dent).

obsessions, even at times manias, and we shall not go into them here. Nevertheless, we must observe that these distracting subjective elements not only prevented him from achieving the architecture of the Finale but also invaded its material—and this was fatal to his instinctive desire for the kind of last movement that would once more reach objectivity. In these pathetic relics we find the *débris* of the last battle between Bruckner and the fiend of nervous subjectivity he had fought all his life, and often beaten with triumphant decisiveness. It would not be fair to say he lost the final contest, for he simply did not live to finish it. But the fight was far from won, and his faculties would not allow him freedom of action. We can see from the very first idea in these sketches that the material itself, full of originality and unlike anything in the openings of previous finales, has a strangely obsessive quality. Hitherto Bruckner has always begun a finale with a clearly shown sense of direction, even when the air is full of mystery; here he is fascinated by a remarkable harmonic sensation (fixation, almost) from which he finds it difficult to escape convincingly into larger areas:

Ex 1

Later we come across a chorale that, while it is obviously not intended to play as large a part in the structure as the one in the Fifth Symphony, is clearly meant to provide an affirmative element. But by no feat of wishful thinking can it be said to match the one in the Fifth either in melodic distinction or in tensile strength; it is a mere skeleton, and there is no knowing how Bruckner might have altered it at a later stage. I quote its beginning in the convenient form shown in Redlich's introduction to the Eulenburg miniature score (Ex. 2, overleaf).*

When Bruckner knew that he might not finish the Ninth he suggested that the *Te Deum* could be used as a finale, and the presence in the sketches of a motive (the figuration that is heard in quavers at the outset of the choral work) led to the supposition that he was composing

* Edited by Hans-Hubert Schönzeler; this is the most accurate edition.

Ex 2

some kind of link between the two works. There is no evidence to suggest that Bruckner, even in the poor state of health and mind of his last few months of life, considered the use of the C major *Te Deum* as finale to a D minor symphony to be more than a makeshift solution, and certainly none to justify the idea that he would contemplate anything so inorganic as a modulatory transition between the two. In any case, his habit of self-quotation was long ingrained, and this is sufficient explanation of the presence of the *Te Deum* figure, itself a type so characteristic that it could have occurred spontaneously. The fact that he labelled it "Te Deum" in the sketches simply shows that the quotation was deliberate, not that it was to be used in a link.

In this book, however, we are concerned with Bruckner's positive achievement rather than with conjecture about his unfulfilled intentions, interesting and even moving though such a study can be, and we had better consider the completed movements without further delay. The vast opening is essentially a long *crescendo*, containing a number of ideas, culminating in a tremendous unison establishing D minor. We have already observed (see p. 67) that this *crescendo* process is twice the size of that at the start of the Third Symphony, and this means that there can be no question of delivering it again immediately with a new tonal direction, as happens in No. 3. And it is even less comparable than the earlier beginning with that of Beethoven's Ninth. The procession of themes and slow "lapidary" accumulation create a kind of

momentum that is remotely alien from Beethoven's. Where Beethoven
rapidly increases the tension by a progressive tightening of the rhythm
so that the main theme has greater impetus than its preparation (a
characteristic of sonata organization, for the rest of the movement is
thereby impelled forward), Bruckner's "main" theme is near the end of a
procession, which it brings to a halt. We have time to pause and look
back. As in the Third Symphony, moreover, Bruckner makes certain
that D minor is the key from the outset, and the solemn chant-like
horn theme that looms out of the dark is itself almost as self-contained
as the trumpet theme in the earlier symphony. And when (in bar 19)
the music flares out into a foreign key, the tension created is of the
opposite kind from Beethoven's; the latter crowds his idea fiercely
upon the expectations, while Bruckner's tension results from what is
essentially a delaying action. The whole massive paragraph from the
beginning to the aftermath of the climax consequently occupies no
less than 96 bars of very moderate tempo, during which we form the
impression of a single idea of colossal slowness. Here are the eight main
thematic elements contained in it:

Already we must accept the fact that although we may discover contrasting themes and sections, and a large-scale use of related or unrelated tonal areas, it would be foolish to expect sonata behaviour. In fact this first movement is one of the few individual Bruckner designs that is more or less describable by simple terminology, and it will save great confusion if we notice that the whole movement divides into two main sections (which we can label Statement and Counter-statement) with a huge but simple *coda* added. The first thing to realize, however, is that the mighty opening passage is itself only a segment of the vast Statement; the opening itself has numerous passing tonal inflexions that are not radical modulations and do not shake the stony domination of D minor—the motion has barely begun. The passage based on Ex. 3 (h) is only reluctantly a transition, and at the last moment it seems to halt on the dominant of a foreign key (E flat); but this proves to be a German sixth that resolves on A major. Even so the drum and the violas still softly underline D, and the drum, indeed, carries its D over into the A major chord at bar 97; this may possibly be an oversight on Bruckner's part, if he intended the D to drop to A— on the other hand it may be a symptom of the persistence of D itself. If the latter is Bruckner's idea, it must be confessed less than adequately pointed. At all events the key of D is massively grounded: where some

other Bruckner movements evolve by tonal disputation, or by searching for a tonic (as does the *Adagio* of this symphony) this one is remorselessly pinned down by its basic key—no other is able convincingly to
challenge it.

The Statement continues with a flowing new theme in A major;
the tempo is slower, the mood nobly reflective:

Ex 4 (bar 97)

Langsamer

Tonally the music is very restless, however, and in bars 105–9 we
find quietly hopeful F sharp major phrases sternly answered by D
minor, but later (bar 115) we rise into the bright light of E major, the
dominant of A. Passing through F sharp minor we reach an aspiring
new melody, *forte*, in C major (letter E); but there is something forced
about it, and soon there is a return to Ex. 4, again in A major. This
time comes a gain in confidence and Ex. 4 sings like a rich chorale over
a climax on the dominant of D flat, falling away in mystery. On the
dominant of D flat an oboe gives out another new idea (bar 153); a
horn answers it in A minor and the mystery deepens—so does a sense
of the ominous. Yet we settle on the dominant of A (bar 161).

So far we have had two tonal centres, an absolutely unequivocal
D minor, driven home by the whole of Ex. 3, and a less than sure A
major, arising from Ex. 4. The fact that there was something unreal
about the would-be radiance of A major is now crushingly confirmed
by another theme—in D minor. It is a coldly severe inversion of the
oboe idea from bar 153:

Ex 5 (bar 167)

Moderato

Vlns

This is the third stage of the Statement. Ex. 5 gloomily rises to a
counterstatement of its own (bar 179), still in a dismal D minor, then
it shifts its ground as the melody begins sluggishly to develop, the
horns adding a solemnly laboured counterpoint. In G flat comes a
somewhat Brahmsish line that should be noted:

Ex 6 (bar 191)

The whole system strains and pushes towards a heavy earthbound climax that clears, at the last moment, into F major. The whole of this paragraph has a weary air. Not only is it the expression of spiritual lassitude, but it is, I am certain, the result of actual tiredness of body and mind, and becomes not merely weary but dangerously wearisome as it hauls itself towards its somewhat crudely scored apex. We must never forget, in criticizing the Ninth, that the whole of what is extant is only its first draft, that Bruckner would certainly have gone over it all again. But the F major that follows all this rather flabby protesting is magical; the close of the Statement is in an atmosphere of strange hallucinatory elation, enhanced by the weird B natural that flickers through the soft veil of sound.

To call this gigantic Statement an exposition would be literally correct, since it exposes all the main matter, but it is better to avoid terminology with misleading associations. Commentators have usually attempted to describe what follows as a sort of combination of development and recapitulation. No doubt the composer himself would have done so, but we can understand what he is instinctively aiming at by more clearly and simply realizing that it is a colossal expansion of the opening *crescendo* (finally confirming the impossibility of immediately counterstating the opening) followed by a telescoping of the two succeeding sections (Exx. 4–6), the whole to be an Expanded Counterstatement. Beginning at bar 229 over a pedal F, the music grows in four immense waves to the unison theme (Ex. 3 (f), itself magnified into two even larger sweeps, the first (bar 333) enveloped in furious titanic string passages and the second (bar 355) tramping and heaving towards a truly seismic irruption in F minor—here the music can be matched in words only by the power of Milton:

> Forthwith upright he* rears from off the pool
> His mighty stature; on each hand the flames
> Driven backward slope their pointing spires, and, rolled
> In billows, leave i' the midst a horrid vale.
>   * Satan (*Paradise Lost*, Book I).

Then with expanded wings he steers his flight
Aloft, incumbent on the dusky air,
That felt unusual weight; till on dry land
He lights—if it were land that ever burned
With solid, as the lake with liquid fire,
And such appeared in here as when the force
Of subterranean wind transports a hill
Torn from Pelorus, or the shattered side
Of thundering Ætna, whose combustible
And fuelled entrails, thence conceiving fire,
Sublimed with mineral fury, aid the winds,
And leave a singèd bottom all involv'd
With stench and smoke. Such resting found the sole
Of unblest feet.

After this, slow gently circling figures disperse the terror and drift
into the consolatory second part of the Counterstatement; the transition itself is a little weak and automatic in its sequential repetitions and
augmentations, as if the previous mighty effort had tired the composer.
But the return of Ex. 4 in D major is a fine relief, at any rate for a
while. The aspiring theme from letter E is now made to appear in
B flat rather than in F (which has been volcanically erupted by the
previous climax) and it now leads, not without some awkward stiffness
of phrase and harmony, to Ex. 5, which emerges in the unexpected
key of B minor (bar 459). Soon, however, it slips back to the old D
minor, and drags itself up to a dissonant climax, more stridently complaining than ever, saturated with overripe harmony and scoring that
clog rather than intensify its movements. The climax itself (letter W)
batters obstreperously for ten bars of a rhythmic obviousness that is
scarcely supportable. I feel sure that some of my fellow devotees will
want my blood for thus describing what, for all I know, may be a
favourite passage, but am equally sure that Bruckner would have
paused and pondered over it in any revision he might later have been
able to carry out. When it has mercifully desisted, a genuinely impressive cadential passage in woodwind and brass descends darkly to the
home dominant, and it is time for the *coda*. As always with Bruckner,
this is masterly and awesome. For it he has reserved the chorale-like
figure Ex. 3 (g), which has not been heard at all since its first appearance
as a grand cadence to the mighty unison theme. A stupendous black
cavern of sound is created as it forms the last *crescendo*, containing also

the ghosts of Ex. 3 (b) and (f). The end is a terrible hollow fifth, against which Ex. 3 (b) grinds fearsomely on the flat supertonic with all the minatory force (and perhaps in Bruckner's mind the literal meaning) of a *Dies irae*.

Enormous as this design is, it would be extremely terse were it not for the passage between bars 277 and 301, where the vast expansion of the original opening *crescendo* is interrupted by a somewhat abortive and irrelevant reference to Ex. 6; this, too, Bruckner might well have reconsidered at the stage of revision. A cut would certainly not do, for the composer's instinct for proportion is right, and although a cut from L to M would restore the natural sequence of ideas, the whole passage would then be too short. Only the composer could have solved this difficulty. Nevertheless the conciseness of the movement, despite this and other inequalities, should not be overlooked; it is an error to assume that conciseness and brevity are inseparable. Is an elephant less concise than a flea? It is all a question of proportion, and mastery of movement and design. In art, as in biology, sufficiency is all; there must be no understatement (how often is this word used in praise when "suggestion" is meant!) or exaggeration. The prime requirement, whether the proportions be small or large, is exactitude. The kind of precision we find in Bruckner's most perfect work is not quite achieved in either the first movement or the *Adagio* of the Ninth—but for all we can tell, they may simply be less unfinished than the Finale.

The foregoing description is not more than an outline of the general shape of the first movement, and we should not leave it without looking in a little more detail at it from the beginning of the Counterstatement onwards. The ending of the Statement in F major (bar 227) coincides with the start of the immensely expanded Counterstatement. The music stays in F as Ex. 3 (a) returns in various *stretti* with itself in inverted augmentation. Needless to say, no contrapuntal skill is required to make this theme involve itself in any kind of texture—but Bruckner's ear is always sensitive in such a situation and his sense of slow movement is here unfailing, so that the music creates a feeling of awe. The strings add a portentous new counterpoint in slow minims (bar 229). Then the bass moves from F to G flat (bar 239), and Ex. 3 (a) grows into (b), which blazes majestically to the dominant of F sharp (bar 252) (this brass passage, whenever it occurs, is like the effect of turning abruptly from an interior of sepulchral gloom to a magnificent stained-glass window). At the end of bar 252 the woodwind begin Ex. 3 (a) again on the note A; the previous harmony leads the ear to expect F sharp minor, but instead A minor is the key. Second violins and cellos join with an inversion of (c) while first violins play a free diminution of the same figure (its shape completely altered but its rhythmic basis unmistakable). Once more the music moves deliberately to (b), now pausing on the dominant of A (bar 276). If the key of A is adumbrated so pointedly, the tonic D cannot be far off.

At bar 277 comes the irrelevance based on Ex. 6 (mentioned earlier); the strings (*pizzicato*) play a free augmentation of Ex. 4 (a) and the whole complex, having frustrated the dominant of A by returning to F, erects a rather mechanical *crescendo* to the dominant of D flat and halts at bar 301. A curious result of this passage is to reveal that the figuration begun by the second violins in bar 303 is an inversion of Ex. 4 (b)—but it was also a derivative of Ex. 3 (c) (refer back to the melodically different but rhythmically identical figure, first violins, bar 253), so Ex. 3 (c) and Ex. 4 (a) are now connected. Subtle ingenuities of this kind can give great pleasure, and this one goes some way towards compensating for the inapt and somewhat helpless passage between L and M. It cannot, of course, justify it, for the second violin figure at bar 303 would still, even without the intervening episode, have been firmly connected with the quaver figuration after letter K, while the new and more purposeful treatment of Ex. 3 (c) beginning in C major at bar 305 would certainly have balanced the contradiction of the expected key of A, as well as maintained the natural growth of the whole paragraph. But, as we have seen, a cut would make the whole seem truncated.

From K onwards Ex. 3 (c) dominates a *crescendo*, moving inevitably into (e) with the octave figure of (d) present in the woodwind and the quaver figuration transferred to the bass. It culminates as before in (f) in D minor, now in a great stormy *tutti* that modulates in seven-league strides to the remotest possible threshold (that of A flat). With a menacing slower tempo the second wave of the central climax commences in A flat minor (bar 355); Ex. 3 (a) is concentrated into heavy treading crotchets (strings) against many strange versions of (f), becoming more and more terrifying and at length reaching the shattering F minor climax at bar 391.

The whole gigantic passage from J to R is thus an expanded counter-statement of the matter of Ex. 3, with the single redundancy referred to, and it is perhaps as well that we have reserved close examination of it until after it has been noticed in broad fact. The trouble with many attempts to analyse Bruckner is that they take insufficient note

of the larger aspects and look for conventional explanations in a mass
of detail. It is no use trying to make distinctions between recapitulatory
and developmental elements in such music; a counterstatement
expanded as far as this must inevitably involve development, and it
must also employ a new tonal scheme.

The rest of the Counterstatement and the *coda* we have already
described enough to set the reader looking for more detail. Notice that
the F minor upheaval at bar 391 is tonally poised on a 6/4 chord, and
that the C on the drum drops mysteriously to an A *natural* which
becomes eventually the home dominant. The key of F, in fact,
vehement though its assertion in the minor has been, is still not
allowed to undermine the central D minor of the movement, and
when Ex. 4 returns in D major, it is as if the tonic had never been
disturbed.

If the first movement is a kind of *Dies irae*, the Scherzo is the business
of the fiendish attendants of those found wanting. Bruckner himself
does not seem so personally involved as in the preceding movement,
and there is a potent detachment and objectivity here—evil depicted
by one who is himself unsoiled. The music is of astonishing originality,
and although the key is still D minor, the dissonant opening proves
itself to be a kind of intensified dominant only when the first *tutti*
breaks out fiercely in a tonic that gathers the harshness into itself in a
peculiarly diabolical way:

Like all Bruckner's large scherzos it is in concentrated sonata form,
and is virtually monothematic, though the curling quaver line in
second violins at letter B becomes important. Notice the powerful
inversions rising out of the bass from letter D onwards, and the
extraordinary savagery of the orchestral writing in bars 97–104; both
these elemental passages are violently aggravated in the recapitulation.
The exposition ends in A minor, and the development begins *piano*

with a mocking A major transformation of the main theme on an oboe; an air of false frivolity invades the music, unprecedented in Bruckner, and it grows. We almost begin to believe in it when the smiling face freezes horrifyingly into a mask (see bar 147 *et seq.*). The infernal gates are flung open, and the monstrous Ex. 7 flies out. The recapitulation outdoes everything else in ferocity and ends in a devilish din of D minor.

The icy Trio is a complete reversal of Bruckner's normal practice; it is at a much faster tempo than the Scherzo. It both compels and repels as it snakes quickly across the scene, and there is nothing like it elsewhere in this composer's music, or perhaps in any other's. It is in F sharp major and is almost in itself a scherzo and trio. The first part, beginning and ending in the tonic, has two themes, the first in spidery *staccato* quavers beginning in the fifth bar, and the second smooth and harmonically slippery at bar 53. Here the more slyly feline evils of that Place abound, and also in the shuddering heart of the piece (between letters D and F). Snakes, spiders, cats—no, we do injury to these innocent creatures by comparing them with the nameless things that slide through this music. It is almost a relief when the honest ravening of the Scherzo returns.

The *Adagio* is the most tortuous music Bruckner ever wrote. It is a search for a way out of the terrors and horrors of the first two movements and it is at the same time a search for a tonality, beginning with an agonized minor ninth that twists back on itself to an equally distressed major seventh. The desolation is then softened by harmony, and the melody struggles upwards through a chord of D major, and then further, to the dominant of A:

Ex 8
Langsam, feierlich

Darkness returns, but still the upward urge remains, and the light brightens mysteriously until it flames in a wonderful chord on the dominant of B, with the horns transforming the minor ninth of

Ex. 8 (a) into a major ninth, and the trumpets sounding strange fragmentary fanfares. This is one of the most remarkable and perfectly realized sounds in all Bruckner's music. But the brilliance fades as the harmony shifts to the dominant of B flat (bar 25). Horns and tubas are left to sound a mournful chorale in B flat minor (over a dominant pedal) which moves to 6/4 harmony on A major, and thence down another step into the clouded dominant of A flat. So far no single tonality has had security. Despondency reigns.

Now for the first time we hear an expected key, and in A flat comes a new melody. Superficially it belongs to the same family as Ex. 11 in the First Symphony or Ex. 8 in the Seventh (see p. 36 and p. 149) but though it purports to be consoling, there is something forlorn and wintry in it, partly due to the parsimony of its scoring:

Ex 9 (bar 45)

It clings for a time to A flat major; then at bar 57 the strings, with a change to G flat, attempt to soar:

Ex. 10 (bar 57)

They reach clearer air and in a much warmer A major, Ex. 9 comes back. But the light dims again and a solitary flute is left tracing a thin line over an obscurely alien dominant. We cannot possibly realize it at present, but it is the threshold (in the form of a German sixth) of the key the music will finally discover. The first theme returns and already its opening B has a dominant sound, as if in faint realization that E major is what it is looking for. But the way is again missed. This time the dominant of A (bar 83—this is emphatically not the key of E major, any more than it was at bar 7) is followed by C sharp minor and a weirdly expressive mirror-combination of the first two bars of the theme with its own image. This time the subject climbs to the dominant of B, and in B minor the inversion of Ex. 8 (a) revolves about its own axis in a melancholy-majestic *fortissimo*, with tramping scales beneath and restless wide-leaping syncopations above. The tonality is raised in effortful steps, B, C, D, E flat, E, F and at bar 101 there is a mystified hush, and the same phrase, still inverted, is heard in a strange harmonic atmosphere, which the bassoon, at the end of bar 104, timidly identifies as the dominant of E (it is notated in flats).

But the strings fail to receive the message and at letter G the cellos, playing Ex. 8 (a) the right way up, begin to explore G major. This initiates another climbing process, and slow sequences labour upwards to the extraordinarily luminous major-ninth harmony first heard at bar 17, but now on the dominant of C; as if aware that this is the wrong direction it quietens and darkens into a more apprehensively dissonant chord, and there is a pause. Now, for a while, it seems as if Bruckner himself is groping—a different matter from skilfully and subtly ordering the groping of the music. Again we must remember that this score may not have been the definitive conception, and, as Bruckner brings in Ex. 10, seemingly trying out A flat again, we may well wonder if he would not have reconsidered its *non sequitur* and its ill-starred attempt to soar to somewhere or other. He might perhaps have newly composed the rather laboured sequential growth from bar 105 to its climax at bar 121, cut out the interpolation of Ex. 10 and joined K to J. Though I would not advocate a cut (and indeed would wrathfully condemn the impudence) I do not think the proportions would have suffered if Bruckner had omitted the passage between J and K, and the following treatment of Ex. 8 (b) would be harmonically natural after the pause at J, as well as being the next segment of the main theme due for development.

Ex. 8 (b) now strains upward, becoming increasingly intense, and the stern brass create a sense of doom as their sharp descending thrusts cut across the rising chromatic phrases. Then the woodwind dispel the fear with soft new light on the same material, in C major at first, and bring about a beautiful variant of the horn and tuba chorale from bar 29, originally so funereal, now radiant in the strings (letter L). The harmony is kaleidoscopic, but settles at bar 163 in G flat, as far away from C major as possible. A new passage begins, full of expectancy, treating Ex. 8 (a) and wheeling harmonically with a shrouded hint of reassurance. Then, in an immensely slow tempo, Ex. 9 returns, and we are at last in E major.

Hitherto a Bruckner slow movement has invariably built its last great *crescendo* on the main theme; now he departs from this habit by evolving it from the second, which has not been recapitulated. The

G

tempo here can hardly be too slow, given a fine orchestra finely conducted, and the whole passage has a supreme inevitability, a mighty grandeur, and an originality of harmony that surpasses any possible description. Its enormous culmination, however, is far from the affirmation we are led to expect. Ex. 8 (a) suddenly emerges calamitous and vast, surrounded by an affrighting halo of dissonance; the summit is an alarming chord that so shocked Ferdinand Loewe that he diluted it in his notorious falsification of the score after the composer's death. (We have not discussed this edition, which is still obtainable but which should never be performed; Loewe conducted his version in 1903, without indicating that it was not Bruckner's own, and the enormity of its alterations in scoring and harmony, none of which could possibly have been made with the composer's consent, are final proof of the lamentable quality of the advice with which Bruckner was for so many years plagued. The crime in this particular case was the publication of this false score in 1903 and the suppression of the original until 1934, after the deaths of Loewe and Franz Schalk.)

This fearsome consummation of the *crescendo* is, despite its harshness, plainly on the dominant of C sharp minor, and the gentle pleading reaction from it, softly turning away wrath and the threatened tonality, is the beginning of the most beautiful and sensitive of all Bruckner's quiet codas. Opening with a literal recapitulation of the passage that began at bar 9, it begins to swell, but instead of arriving at the massive major ninth on the dominant of B (as it did at bar 17), it moves into a new and hushed benedictory version of Ex. 9 (a), descending with great and delicately unsentimental innocence to E major and a reminiscence of the *Adagio* of the Eighth, of deeper serenity than anything in that. The very close is another memory, of the opening of the Seventh Symphony. So ends Bruckner's uncompleted life's work; though we may regret the absence of the vast background to all this that might have been disclosed by an achieved finale, we may be grateful that this last *Adagio*, though it is not his most perfect, is his most profound.

CHAPTER XI

REFLECTIONS

Writing of Nielsen in 1952* the thought occurred to me that this Danish master, were it not for the humane single-mindedness and clarity of his outlook on life, might well have fallen victim to his own versatility. That he did not do so is a mark of his stature. Bruckner, a less comprehending and comprehensive artist both humanly and musically, was never exposed to that danger; he spent most of his creative life in the solving of one set of problems, in the pursuit of which his instincts were sometimes at war with his prejudices. Although he was not versatile, his problems and his instincts led him into a variety of attempts and solutions, so that his symphonies are in reality much more diverse in character and form than would appear to the superficial critic. His originality is beyond question, and out-standing even in an age when individuality was avidly sought; yet it is doubtful if Bruckner ever tried consciously to be original. It is more likely that for many years he was deeply concerned to prove himself orthodox and competent, in his own eyes as well as those of others—his lifelong desire for testimonials of all kinds is evidence of this. It is probable that in his most imaginatively new designs he was endeavour-ing simply to expand classical conventions. So far as his conscious mentality was concerned he was a much more conventional musician than Brahms, who outgrew an early fascination for Liszt and Wagner (for the latter, indeed, Brahms had a more than sneaking respect all his life). Bruckner never ceased to abase himself before Wagner's music, but he must have understood it in a general sense much less than Brahms, who was its official enemy. It is fortunate that Bruckner's grasp of Wagner was less than complete, for he might have gone the way of many another composer if he had too easily been able to reproduce its typical features and processes. But in every respect save that of fatally accurate imitation, Bruckner was Wagner's slave. Brahms was no one's, and his conscious wish to preserve the power of classical music made him the god of the conservatives. The atmosphere became such that the two men could not meet without strain. When we consider the situation from our safe distance, a great irony reveals

* *Carl Nielsen, Symphonist* (Dent, 1952).

itself: Bruckner, the conventional, provincial Austrian musician and almost abjectly devout Catholic, completely bemused by Wagner; Brahms, an intellectual of the highest powers, agnostic, subtle, profoundly German, yet openly antagonistic to Wagner. But Bruckner and Brahms had more in common than either ever realized.

These two composers, very differently, sought to find new ways of continuing the classical symphonic tradition, and it is demonstrable that Brahms, though his symphonies are more obviously in line with Haydn, Mozart and Beethoven, was in many ways the less orthodox of the two, mainly because he had no difficulty in understanding the manifold unorthodoxies of the great classical composers. It is arguable that Bruckner was more aware of classical patterns in the abstract than of the intricate individualities of classical practice. The result was that his own strange and potent instinct was undistracted by the subtleties that sometimes made Brahms self-critical to the point of despair. Bruckner's distractions were caused by intellectuals and by ideas he could not understand; Brahms's were caused by those he could. Brahms, whatever antagonisms he may have expressed, understood Wagner; Bruckner, whatever adoration he showed, did not. Bruckner was bowled over by the sound of Wagner's music, but did not know what it really meant, whereas Brahms, resisting its heady appeal, knew and resented its significance. It is likely that Brahms was contemptuous of Bruckner not because the latter admired Wagner, but because Bruckner's admiration was patently without analytic understanding. Dvořák, after all, never concealed his love of Wagner, but this did not prevent Brahms from becoming one of his strongest advocates. Bruckner's laborious erudition in academic counterpoint and harmony must have struck Brahms as pedantry of the stupidest kind, myopically insensible of the sort of life-giving subtlety he adored in Mozart or Beethoven. It is not surprising that Bruckner's symphonies struck Brahms as unholy monsters, cross-bred between incompatibles and further deformed by inexpert midwifery. Yet if Brahms had taken a more sympathetic interest in what Bruckner was really doing, he would have found plenty of subtlety of a kind to understand, and might well have seen that Bruckner's instinct was in its way as perceptive as his own. Their attitudes to Wagner divided them; yet they had more in common with each other than either had, in truth, with his own supporters in the feud. There is evidence that Brahms came at last to an inkling of this, for he was seen to applaud vigorously a performance of Bruckner's F minor mass and afterwards persuaded the conductor,

Richard von Perger, to perform the *Te Deum*. This is more than Bruckner's beloved Wagner ever did for him. Given a few more years, Brahms might well have come to see the virtues of Bruckner's symphonies.

The Brahms-Wagner opposition did more harm to Bruckner than to anyone. Most of his admirers were ardent Wagnerians who were keen to use him as a stick to beat Brahms. There was no other symphonist of any stature at that time who could be press-ganged into the rôle. When Dvořák came forward, his earlier Wagnerian works were still unknown and the heat of the battle had cooled. Dvořák, in any case, was moving into the Brahmsian ambit. Bruckner, moreover, was naïve and malleable; he could easily be persuaded that his music needed certain adjustments to make it "go down", and perhaps did not sense that such adjustments were often made with specifically Wagnerian motives. In saying this, we must not fall into the old error of accusing these advisers of ruthless and calculated distortion of the music for nefarious ulterior motives. There can be no doubt that the Schalk brothers, Ferdinand Loewe, and others genuinely believed they were of real assistance to Bruckner. His simplicity led them to think they were helping him discover his own dimly perceived intentions. The trouble is that they were wrong. Although the composer himself did in fact have no more than the dimmest explainable idea of his own goal, their conception of it, though lucid to themselves, was a complete misunderstanding based on what they found in Wagner. Their championship of Bruckner antagonized many who might have understood him better than they, and their copious advice, far from reassuring the timid composer, threw him into agonies of uncertainty and protracted bouts of revising, without which he might have written much more music. As a result of their labours, Bruckner was for decades misapprehended as a Wagnerian symphonist. They had little idea of symphonic construction (Franz Schalk's version of the Finale of the Fifth is typically crass), and their notions of Wagner's own methods were rudimentary—for they saw nothing wrong with "bleeding chunks" from the music dramas, so long as their edges were decently trimmed. But we have seen some of the results of their aid to Bruckner in the foregoing chapters and there is no need to continue the tale. It is a pity that there are still those who are prepared to perpetuate the confusion by using musicological pedantry where only insight will do; as we have frequently seen, the facts are often impossible to find out by normal scientific research methods.

The essence of Bruckner's music, I believe, lies in a patient search for pacification. This does not mean a mystical longing for "peace", and I do not share the view that only a religious man (and some would insist, even, only an Austrian Catholic) can understand Bruckner. If that were so his work would be abhorrent to many (including myself) who love it. Bruckner's devoutness in the Catholic faith was one of his few defences against a world he was mentally and psychologically ill-fitted to face; as he became less able to defend himself, so it developed more surely into religious mania. His natural timorousness and his upbringing in the almost feudal conditions of nineteenth-century pastoral Austria, under the stern authoritarianism of the church, made it almost impossible for him to be other than what he became. This means, of course, that his music often expresses the emotional condition of religious conviction, but that cannot be said to be its essence any more than were the sonata forms he sometimes must have thought he was creating. There is something in Bruckner's art that appeals to mentalities unsympathetic to his religious beliefs as much as it does to those that share them. Each side will accuse the other of misunderstanding it, or of trying to explain it by special pleading; the religious man will say that the infidel who is profoundly moved by Bruckner is touched by religious instincts he is unprepared to admit, while the heretic will reply that the other is placing a religious or mystical interpretation on matters that originate otherwise. I have already indicated which side I am on. Ignoring my own sympathies, it seems to me an incontrovertible fact that neither side is able to prove to the other that it derives the deeper and more satisfactory experience from the music, and I cannot help wondering how much of this argument would have flourished if nothing had been known about Bruckner's personal life. One thing is certain—the artistic problems with which he wrestled, whatever their psychic origins, produced characteristic artistic phenomena appreciable by people of directly and profoundly opposed beliefs. It is these phenomena this book has been concerned with, and I do not think this to be an evasion of the issue, for art and biography have often proved contradictory.

By speaking of a search for pacification in Bruckner's music I mean its tendency to remove, one by one, disrupting or distracting elements, to seem to uncover at length a last stratum of calm contemplative thought. The supreme achievement of this kind is the Eighth Symphony, in which the movements seem successively to reveal each other. The stormy turbulence of the first movement having passed, we perceive in the Scherzo the energy behind it; when that is spent, the *Adagio* slowly and often with effort uncovers the serene and powerful Finale. It is difficult to explain in words what the music itself explains in its own terms. I am sure that the characteristic Brucknerian process is essentially the reverse of the kind which raises the tension until it explodes into a finale. Human tensions in Bruckner are usually gradually pacified, and this is a positive, not a negative, process; they are at once balanced, directed, and strengthened in the Finale of the Eighth, and in this Bruckner differs radically from the type of romantic who relieves rather than calms his own tensions. In every one of Bruckner's symphonies except the First and the Seventh we find this tendency towards gradual pacification. Sometimes the disturbing elements themselves are allowed to develop slowly during the course of a symphony, as in the Sixth, where the process results in mysterious disclosures. But even here the tensions, although they are bared for the first time in the Finale, at length achieve a fine balance—at no time is there any feeling that the music is driving towards some all-embracing emotional climax. The massive endings of all Bruckner's symphonies are (with the exception of that of the Fifth) not really culminative in the old sense; they are formal intensifications that blaze with calm. Even in the Fifth there is ultimately this sense of a calm fire, and the last movement of the Seventh, though it activates rather than quiets the energies of the symphony as a whole, creates more an equilibrium than a dramatic *dénouement*. When a Bruckner finale is not successful it is not because it fails to achieve an accumulative climax in relation to the rest of the symphony; it is because the process of pacification has become dangerously near petrification. He has failed, not to resolve conflicting tensions in a burst of unidirectional energy, but to balance them in a statuesque structure.

The quality most notable in the search for such an expression is patience, and this is what I think Bruckner's music really defines. In emphasizing the need for patience in both understanding and performing Bruckner, and for pointing out that this quality is indeed one of the chief things his music expresses, I have been accused of a somewhat priggish form of special pleading.* But patience is a state of mind, and I doubt if there is any state of mind music cannot express. Love music demands from its hearers a knowledge (and preferably the experience) of what love is. Patience is, if you like, an aspect of love. It is not easy to cultivate, especially for some people, and it is under-

* "Pecksniffian" was the kindly term employed.

standable that music born of and expressing patience might well be too much for some mentalities, which cannot be blamed for regarding its advocacy in these terms as a kind of moralistic preaching. But if you want to get the most out of Bruckner, you must have great patience in order properly to appreciate it in him. This is neither preaching nor special pleading; it is practical advice, to be taken or left. At his greatest, Bruckner is able to achieve a deep composure, which he can transfer to a receptive listener. The search for this composure is his life's work. It is his search for form, for a new type of symphony that he was never able to rationalize to himself or anyone else, and even his blunders can move while they exasperate us if we comprehend their nature.

All this makes Bruckner really very remote from Wagner. There used to be a legend that Bruckner's symphonies were not only very long but were scored for a *Götterdämmerung*-sized orchestra. In actual fact, he was very slow to absorb Wagner's influence. It was not until the last three symphonies that he brought himself to use Wagner tubas. He never employed even a piccolo or cor anglais, let alone bass flute, bass clarinet, bass trumpet, or contrabass trombone, and he used percussion on only two occasions—the cymbals and triangle in the Seventh and Eighth, in the first case at the instigation of someone else. His idea of the orchestra is positively puritanical compared with Wagner's. The harp he uses but once, in No. 8; he does not return to it in the Ninth. The sound of the Brucknerian orchestra is totally individual, in general plainer than Wagner's and blocked out with massive contrasts. The various sections are often juxtaposed like organ registrations (Tovey pertinently points out that Bruckner's scoring often sounds organ-like because it is entirely free from the mistakes of the organ-loft composer). In his attitude to sonorities Bruckner has more in common with a seventeenth-century master like Giovanni Gabrieli than he has with his own romantic contemporaries. And this is another reflection of his essentially pacific mentality. He is apt to create internal echo effects that demand the depth of a spacious acoustic. Nothing is more damaging to his orchestral imagination than the dry and clinical acoustics of present-day concert halls. The sound of the great church at St. Florian is always in his ears, and the silent pauses he so frequently makes are not really such—they should be filled with awesome reverberation. The opening of the Fifth Symphony is but a shadow of itself in the Royal Festival Hall. If it be held a reprehensible limitation that the music should need special conditions, then not only Bruckner but almost the whole of fifteenth-, sixteenth-, and seventeenth-century church music is punishable. Ultimately every kind of music, from Bach's solo violin partitas to Havergal Brian's Gothic Symphony, requires its own ideal acoustic conditions.

If the influence of Wagner on Bruckner's orchestra is limited, so is it on the substance of his music itself. The earliest marked effect of Wagner is not on its melody or harmony, and certainly not on its structure. At first it is almost entirely undigested, as in the first version (unpublished) of the Third Symphony, which contained open quotations from Wagner, afterwards significantly removed. Later manifestations are confined to occasional Wagnerian fingerprints like the *gruppetto* in Ex. 2 of the Seventh Symphony (see p. 144), or a touch of harmony (see, for instance, bars 337-9 in the Finale of No. 4), or a rhythmic reminiscence (see No. 8, Finale, second tuba, bars 692-3). Such things do not alter Bruckner's unmistakable individuality. On the rare occasions when something like one of Wagner's moods is evoked, as in the Sachs-like wistful kindliness of the coda of the *Adagio* of the Sixth, it is transmuted into something more innocent. (Poor Bruckner was always falling in futile love with young and unsuitable girls whom he could merely worship from a distance; how often must he have felt the poignancy of Hans Sachs's music— presuming he bothered to find out what *Die Meistersinger* was all about!) The beginning of the *Adagio* of No. 9 has often been compared with *Tristan*, and some of its later passages with *Parsifal*, but there is a whole world between the raw direct pain of Bruckner and the subtly powerful sensuality of Wagner. The attempts of his friends to Wagnerize his scores always stand out with dire obviousness against the background of Bruckner's natural character.

Bruckner belonged to the romantic era only in so far as he happened to live in it, sometimes picking up stray influences that appealed to him. He showed a childlike pleasure in encountering anything new and never stopped to ponder its significance in general terms. Occasionally he found its incidental discoveries useful—sounds that interested his musician's curiosity—but not often, for he lived in an inimical world whose products were too often the result of attitudes he could not understand. It is probable that his grasp of the meanings, trends, and processes of society was even less sure than his knowledge of the plot of *The Ring*, almost non-existent. The artistic fashions and movements of his day meant nearly nothing to him as broadly discussable ideas, and what he vaguely perceived he found unsympathetic. To him romanticism meant the naïve "programmes" with which he would sometimes try to interest his up-to-date colleagues in his music; he had little idea of the significance of the passionate arguments he must have heard around him. Bruckner once went to hear a performance of Berlioz's *Damnation of Faust* and was introduced to the composer; the imagination is staggered by the thought—if there were any conversation between the two, what can it possibly have been about? The weather, perhaps, if Bruckner had noticed it. Yet within this oddly humble and puzzled little man was hidden a majesty he discovered for himself with infinite patience and a sublime conscientiousness typical of a great artist. His surroundings and he himself have vanished, and many a sparkling and scornful intellect can bewilder and plague him no more. Though there are Hanslicks still with us, they can no longer trouble him. The frothing tide that often threatened his work and his sanity has long drained into crevices in the soft earth, but the hard and jagged rock of his life's achievement is still there. It has survived all seeming odds. The cracks in the stone are honourable scars on its mighty face.

INDEX

INDEX